CHORDS

FOR
KEYBOARD & GUITAR

**A POCKET REFERENCE GUIDE
TO MORE THAN 1800 CHORDS!**

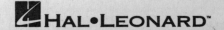

HAL•LEONARD

ISBN 0-7935-4536-6

HAL•LEONARD™
CORPORATION
7777 W. BLUEMOUND RD. P.O. BOX 13819 MILWAUKEE, WI 53213

Contents

Chords and Chord Symbols

A *chord* is usually defined as three or more notes sounding at the same time. Chords provide the *harmony* that supports the melody in a piece of music.

Chords are identified in printed music by *chord symbols*, which appear above the melody line. A chord symbol is an abbreviation for the name of a chord—for example, F♯m7. Chord symbols tell you at a glance what the harmony is.

About this Book

This book is a reference guide to chords, so you can look up a chord symbol easily and find out how to play that chord. It's divided into two parts: one for guitar, the other for keyboard. Each part is arranged as follows:

- **Chords are grouped by root (note name).** Every chord is "built" on a note called the *root*, which gives the chord its letter name. For example, F♯ is the root of F♯m7. In this book you'll find chords grouped by root, starting with C and going up by half steps (D♭/C♯, D, E♭/D♯, etc.) through B.

   (Notice that some notes can be "spelled" in more than one way—e.g., D♭/C♯. This is called *enharmonic equivalence*. This book emphasizes the simplest enharmonic spellings of notes, showing common alternative spellings where they occur.)

- **Within each root, chords are grouped by type.** There are several different *types* of chords, which are identified by the letters and numbers that follow the root in the chord symbol. In F♯m7, the "m7" identifies the chord as a minor seventh type. The following pages explain what these different letters and numbers mean, and how the different types of chords are constructed. But even if you don't care to learn about such things, you can still use this book to look up a particular chord symbol and find what notes you are supposed to play on the guitar or the keyboard.

- **Within each chord type, several different positions are given.** The notes of a chord can be played in any of several different *positions* on the fretboard or the keyboard—that is, arranged in different ways.

   Which position to use depends on the surrounding chords. On guitar, it's often desirable to use chords in a single style or form. On keyboard, it's usually best for chords to move as smoothly as possible from one to the next, with as few large shifts of the hand as possible.

How Chords Are Built

INTERVALS

Chords are built from *intervals*. An interval is the distance between two notes, measured by the number of letter names between them, including the names of the two notes themselves. The following example, a C major scale, identifies the intervals from the bottom C:

Half and Whole Steps

The most important intervals to understand are the *half step* (minor second) and the *whole step* (major second). A half step is the distance from one fret to the next on guitar, or from one key on the keyboard to the next closest key (including black keys). A whole step is two half steps.

TRIADS

The most basic chords have three notes in them. They're called *triads*.

The first note is the *root*. As its name suggests, this note forms the bottom of the chord. For example, let's start with C as a root.

Next comes the *third*, which lies an interval of a third above the root. For a C chord, that would be the note E.

Finally there's the *fifth*, which lies a fifth above the root. For the C chord, the fifth is the note G. Here's the completed chord:

Now, this is how chords are built *in theory*; this is how to figure out what notes a chord contains. But it's not necessarily how the chords are *played*. As mentioned earlier, these notes can be arranged in different positions on the fretboard or keyboard.

Major and Minor

The notes C-E-G spell a C *major* chord. The symbol for this chord is simply the name of the root note—C. It's called a major chord because the third C-E is a *major third*, which equals two whole steps.

If the third of the chord is lowered a half step, to E♭, it becomes a *minor third* (one and a half steps). The resulting chord, C-E♭-G, is called a C *minor* chord. The chord symbol is Cm. (Or Cmi, or C–. Chord names are abbreviated in a variety of ways. This book shows all common symbols for each chord type, giving the most widely used symbol first.)

Sometimes instead of a third, a chord has a *fourth*—technically called a *perfect fourth* (two and a half steps). For a C chord, it would be spelled C-F-G. The chord symbol is Csus4, or just Csus, because the fourth functions as a *suspension*—a dissonant note—that tends to resolve downward to a third.

Guitarists often play "power chords," which consist of just the root and fifth—with no third or fourth. Although it's fewer than three notes, it's still considered a chord. The symbol is C5, or C(no3rd).

The fifth of the chord, by the way, is technically called a *perfect fifth* (three and a half steps). Its presence in the chord is assumed, so it doesn't appear in the chord symbol unless it is *altered*—lowered or raised by a half step—in which case you'll usually see ♭5 or ♯5 in the symbol. For example: C(♭5) (a C major chord with the fifth lowered a half step). Sometimes a lowered or raised fifth entitles a chord to a new name and symbol. (See "Augmented and Diminished," on page 7.)

SIXTHS AND SEVENTHS

The triad is the foundation of all other chords. Other chords consist mostly of notes added to triads.

Adding a sixth above the root (a whole step above the fifth) creates what's called a *sixth* chord. For example: add the sixth, A, to a C chord, and you get a C sixth chord (symbol: C6). Add the sixth to a C minor chord and you get C minor sixth (symbol: Cm6).

The *seventh* is the most common addition to triads. The normal seventh above C is not B, as you might expect, but B♭—sometimes called a *flat seventh*. It's a whole step lower than an octave. Add this to a C chord and you get C seventh— C7; add it to C minor and you get C minor seventh—Cm7; add it to a "sus4" chord and you get C7sus4.

The note B above a C root is called a *major seventh*. Add it to a C chord and you get C major seventh—Cmaj7; add it to a C minor chord and you get C minor, major seventh—Cm(maj7).

AUGMENTED AND DIMINISHED

A couple of chords have their own names, symbols, and rules. The first is the *augmented* chord, which is a triad with a major third and a sharp fifth. Common symbols are C+, Caug, and C(♯5).

Second is the *diminished seventh* chord (often called simply a *diminished* chord), which has a minor third, a flat fifth, and a diminished seventh—a seventh that is lowered a half step from the normal (flat) seventh. Common symbols are Cdim7, Cdim, C°, and C°7. The diminished seventh of this chord is enharmonically equivalent to a sixth—the same note, spelled differently.

Augmented and diminished chords are unusual because the notes are equidistant from one another. Each note in an augmented chord is a major third from the next; each note in a diminished seventh chord is a minor third from the next. This means that in either of these chords, any note can function as the root.

If you add or change any notes in these chords, you change their names and symbols. Take an augmented chord and add a seventh, and its symbol becomes C7♯5. Change a diminished seventh chord so it has a "normal" seventh, and you get Cm7♭5 (infrequently called a *half-diminished* chord, with the symbol C⌀).

NINTHS

Most chords are made up of odd-numbered intervals: root (= "first"), third, fifth, seventh,... This keeps going through ninth, eleventh, and thirteenth. The most common of these larger intervals is the ninth, which is a whole step larger than an octave.

A *ninth* chord—C9, Cm9, C9sus4—actually contains not only the ninth, but the seventh as well. A *major ninth* chord—Cmaj9—contains the ninth and the major seventh.

Sometimes there are more notes in these chords than one hand can reach, so some notes are omitted. For guitar, the fifth is sometimes left out; for keyboard, the root is often the first to go (figuring that a bass player—or another hand—will play it).

Ninths are sometimes lowered or raised by a half step, and this is spelled out in the chord symbol: C7♭9, C7♯9.

A chord with *only* the ninth, and no seventh, is called an *added ninth* chord. The most common is the major triad with added ninth—C(add9)—but you may run into the minor version—Cm(add9).

A major triad with a sixth and a ninth added is a *six-nine* chord—C6/9.

"SLASH CHORDS" AND N.C.

Sometimes a chord symbol ends with a "slash" and an extra letter, like this: C/G. This is used to specify a bass note other than the root of the chord. The example here means "a C chord with the note G in the bass." Often, these bass notes are tones of the chord, such as a third, a fifth, or a seventh, though they may be notes "outside" the chord instead.

You might also see the symbol "N.C." This is an abbreviation for "No Chord," and it means what it says: don't play a chord—until you arrive at the next chord symbol. Sometimes the words "no chord" are written out; sometimes the Latin word "tacet" is used, which means the same thing.

OTHER CHORDS

This book doesn't contain every possible chord; no book does. So what do you do if you run across a chord symbol that isn't spelled out here? Well, you could try to figure out what notes it specifies—and you have a good chance of succeeding, if you understand everything that was explained so far. But there's an easier solution.

Most of the additional chords you'll run across are seventh chords with an added note or two. Leave out the added notes (chances are they appear in the melody anyway) and play the basic version of the chord. The list below tells you which chords to use:

If You See...	Play...
C7♭9, C7♯9, C7♯11, C13	C7
C7♯5(♭9), C7♯5(♯9)	C7♯5
C9sus4, C9sus, C11	C7sus4 (C7sus)
Cmaj7♯11	Cmaj7
Cm11	Cm9

Chord Symbols at a Glance

BASIC SYMBOLS

Symbol:	Chord Type:
C	Major
Cm, Cmin, CMI, C–	Minor
C+, Caug, C(♯5)	Augmented
Cdim, Cdim7, C°, C°7	Diminished Seventh
Cø, Cø7	Half-Diminished Seventh (= Minor Seventh, Flat Fifth)
Csus4, Csus	Suspended Fourth (Instead of Third)
Csus2	Suspended Second (Instead of Third)
C5, C(no3rd)	Power Chord (Without Third)
N.C.	No Chord

ADDITIONS AND ALTERATIONS

Symbol:	Meaning:
6	Sixth
6/9	Sixth and Ninth
7	Flat Seventh
maj7, △7, MA7	Major Seventh
9	Flat Seventh and Ninth
maj9	Major Seventh and Ninth
11	Flat Seventh, Ninth, and Eleventh
13	Flat Seventh, Ninth, Eleventh (optional), and Thirteenth
♭, –	Lower the Following Note by a Half Step
♯, +	Raise the Following Note by a Half Step
add2, add9, add4	Add the Note Specified
C/G	Bass Note other than Root

GUITAR CHORDS CONTENTS

GUITAR CHORDS

FINGERBOARD DIAGRAMS

A *Fingerboard Diagram* (or "frame") is used to show how to play each guitar chord. It pictures a fingerboard with the headstock pointing upward.

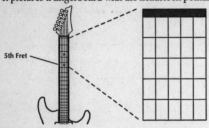

5th Fret

Each diagram focuses on five-fret fragment of the guitar neck, depending on what position a particular voicing is located. The example below shows you how to use a fingerboard diagram:

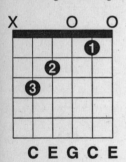

C E G C E

- Vertical lines represent the *strings*
- Horizontal lines indicate the *frets*
- Circles indicate where to press *notes*
- Numerals inside circles indicate proper left hand *fingering* (see next page)
- An "o" placed over a string indicates that the string is played "*open*"
- An "x" placed over string indicates that the string is *not to be played*
- Letters below the strings name the individual *sounding* notes of the particular chord
- A *barre* is shown when a finger holds down two or more strings simultaneously
- *Fret numbers* (e.g. "5 fr") to the right of the first fret are used only if the chord does not fit in the first five frets (if a chord fits in the upper position, a thick top line is used to show the "nut")

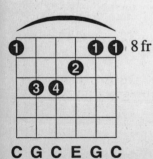

8 fr

C G C E G C

LEFT HAND FINGERS

The fingers of your left hand are numbered
1 through 4, starting with your index finger.

CHOOSING THE BEST VOICING

This book gives you instant access to over 1000 chord voicings. For each
individual chord name, 4 voicings are shown for you to choose from. Although
in theory you may use any of the 4 in any situation, each group does suggest a
specialized function. A chord's location, difficulty, size and intended musical
style all contribute to this determination. Here's how each of the 4 voicings were
chosen and how they should be used:

VOICING #1

The top diagram is the most common *upper position* voicing. It's also the most
appropriate for *strumming* purposes.

VOICING #2

This diagram always gives you a convenient "*all-purpose*" voicing, usable in
most any musical setting.

VOICING #3

Here you'll find another good "all-purpose" voicing, however this voicing is
often a *broken set* form. A broken set chord contains a lower "bass" note and
two or three notes on higher strings with at least one interior string omitted. It
functions best in a jazz or blues setting as a nice "*comping*" (short for
accompaniment) chord.

It is not applicable to show all of the third voicings as broken chords. For those
that are though, pluck them with your fingers (simulating a piano type sound)
or be sure to "mute" out the omitted string as you strum.

VOICING #4

Closed voicing or *adjacent* set chords are used for the fourth group. These often
appear "up the neck" and are of great use in jazz, blues and rock styles.
Although a thinner, less "full" sound results due to the lack of a lower bass note,
it may be more desirable when trying to offset another guitarist or in
complement to the bass player.

C CHORDS

C MAJOR
[C]

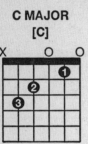

C E G C E

C MINOR
[Cm, Cmi, C-]

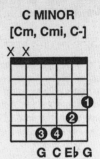

G C E♭ G

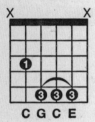

C G C E

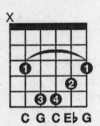

C G C E♭ G

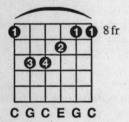

8 fr

C G C E G C

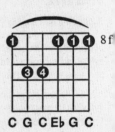

8 fr

C G C E♭ G C

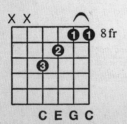

8 fr

C E G C

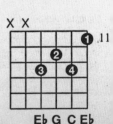

11

E♭ G C E♭

C AUGMENTED
[C+, Caug, C(#5)]

C SUSPENDED FOURTH
[Csus, Csus4]

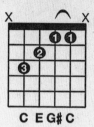

C E G# C

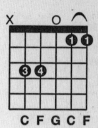

C F G C F

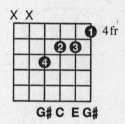

G# C E G#

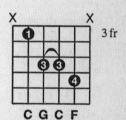

C G C F

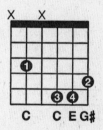

C   C E G#

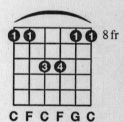

C F C F G C

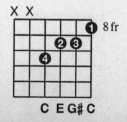

C E G# C

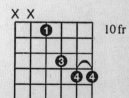

C G C F

C SIXTH
[C6]

C MINOR SIXTH
[Cm6, Cmi6, C-6]

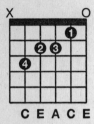

C E A C E

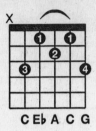

C E♭ A C G

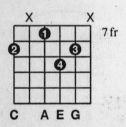

C G C E A

8 fr

C G C E♭ A C

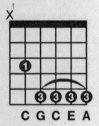

7 fr

C   A E G

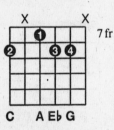

7 fr

C   A E♭ G

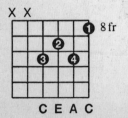

8 fr

C E A C

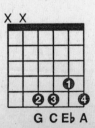

G C E♭ A

C SEVENTH
[C7]

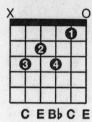

C E B♭ C E

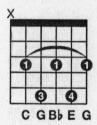

C G B♭ E G

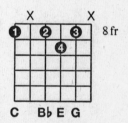

8 fr

C B♭ E G

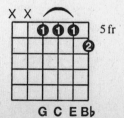

5 fr

G C E B♭

C MAJOR SEVENTH
[Cmaj7, CMA7, C△7]

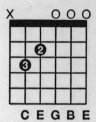

C E G B E

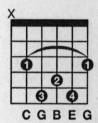

C G B E G

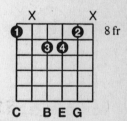

8 fr

C B E G

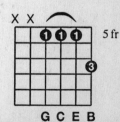

5 fr

G C E B

18

C MINOR SEVENTH
[Cm7, Cmi7, C-7]

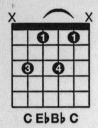

C E♭ B♭ C

C G B♭ E♭ G

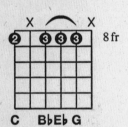

8 fr

C   B♭ E♭ G

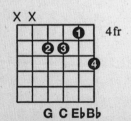

4 fr

G C E♭ B♭

C MINOR MAJOR SEVEN
[Cm(maj7), Cm#7]

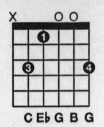

C E♭ G B G

C G B E♭ G

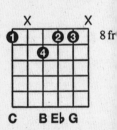

8 fr

C   B E♭ G

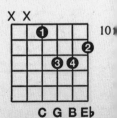

10

C G B E♭

C MINOR SEVENTH FLATTED FIFTH

[Cm7b5, Cmi7b5, C-7b5, C#°7]

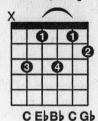

C Eb Bb C Gb

C Gb Bb Eb

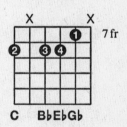

7 fr

C   Bb Eb Gb

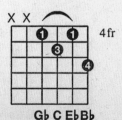

4 fr

Gb C Eb Bb

C DIMINISHED SEVENTH

[Cdim7, C°7, Cdim]

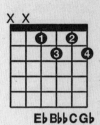

Eb Bbb C Gb

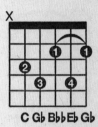

C Gb Bbb Eb Gb

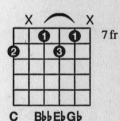

7 fr

C   Bbb Eb Gb

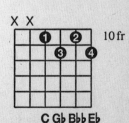

10 fr

C Gb Bbb Eb

C SEVENTH SUSPENDED FOURTH

[C7sus, C7sus4]

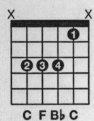

C F Bb C

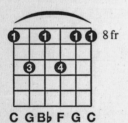

C G Bb F G — 3 fr

C G Bb F G C — 8 fr

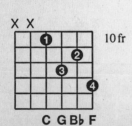

C G Bb F — 10 fr

C SEVENTH SHARPED FIFTH

[C7#5, C+7]

E Bb C G#

C G# Bb E G# — 3 fr

C Bb E G# — 8 fr

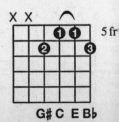

G# C E Bb — 5 fr

C NINTH
[C9]

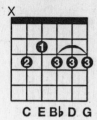

C E B♭ D G

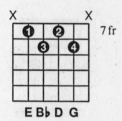

7 fr

E B♭ D G

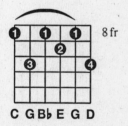

8 fr

C G B♭ E G D

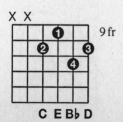

9 fr

C E B♭ D

C MAJOR NINTH
[Cmaj9, CMA9, C△9]

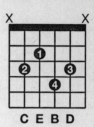

C E B D

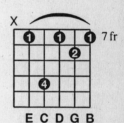

7 fr

E C D G B

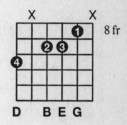

8 fr

D B E G

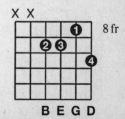

8 fr

B E G D

C MINOR NINTH
[Cm9, Cmi9, C-9]

C ADDED NINTH
[C(add9), C(9), C(add2)]

C Eb Bb D G

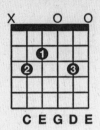

C E G D E

8 fr

C G B Eb G D

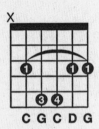

C G C D G

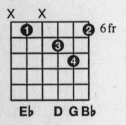

6 fr

Eb D G Bb

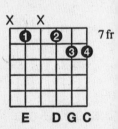

7 fr

E D G C

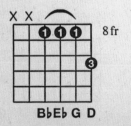

8 fr

Bb Eb G D

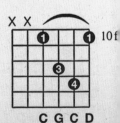

10 fr

C G C D

C SIX NINE
[C6/9, C⁶/9]

C SEVENTH SHARPED NINTH
[C7#9]

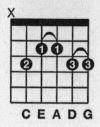

C E A D G

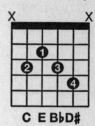

C E B♭ D#

D G C E A

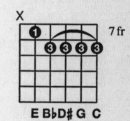

7 fr

E B♭ D# G C

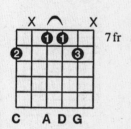

7 fr

C A D G

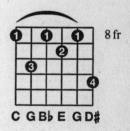

8 fr

C G B♭ E G D#

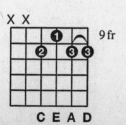

9 fr

C E A D

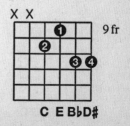

9 fr

C E B♭ D#

C SEVENTH FLATTED NINTH

[C7♭9, C7-9]

C E B♭ D♭

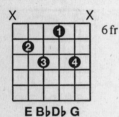

6 fr

E B♭ D♭ G

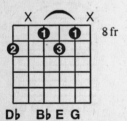

8 fr

D♭ B♭ E G

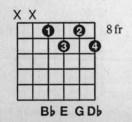

8 fr

B♭ E G D♭

C FIFTH

[C5, C(no3)]

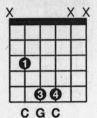

C G C

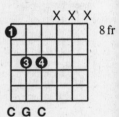

8 fr

C G C

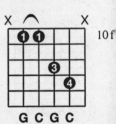

10 fr

G C G C

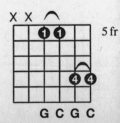

5 fr

G C G C

D♭ CHORDS

D♭ and C♯ are enharmonically equivalent. For the sake of convenience, all chords have been notated as D♭ chords.

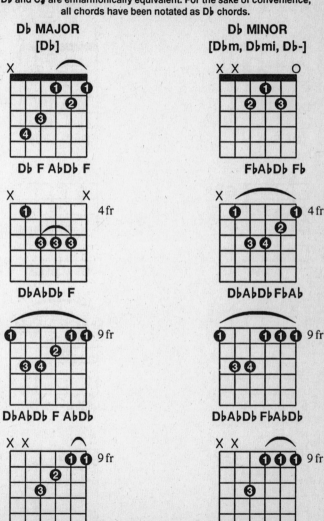

D♭ MAJOR
[D♭]

D♭ F A♭D♭ F

D♭A♭D♭ F

D♭A♭D♭ F A♭D♭

D♭ F A♭D♭

D♭ MINOR
[D♭m, D♭mi, D♭-]

F♭A♭D♭ F♭

D♭A♭D♭F♭A♭

D♭A♭D♭ F♭A♭D♭

D♭ F♭A♭D♭

Db AUGMENTED
[Db+, Dbaug, Db(#5)]

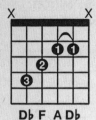

Db F A Db

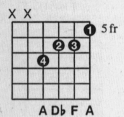

A Db F A

5fr

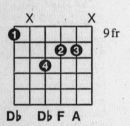

Db Db F A

9fr

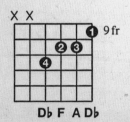

Db F A Db

9fr

Db SUSPENDED FOURTH
[Dbsus, Dbsus4]

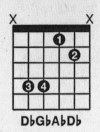

DbGbAbDb

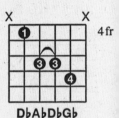

DbAbDbGb

4fr

DbGbDbGbAbDb

9fr

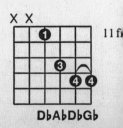

DbAbDbGb

11fr

Db SIXTH
[Db6]

Db MINOR SIXTH
[Dbm6, Dbmi6, Db-6]

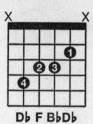

Db F Bb Db

Db Fb Bb Db Ab

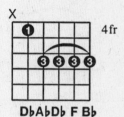

4 fr

Db Ab Db F Bb

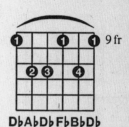

9 fr

Db Ab Db Fb Bb Db

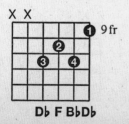

8 fr

Db   Bb F Ab

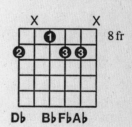

8 fr

Db   Bb Fb Ab

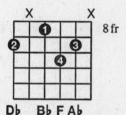

9 fr

Db F Bb Db

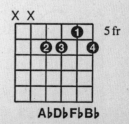

5 fr

Ab Db Fb Bb

Db SEVENTH
[Db7]

Db MAJOR SEVENTH
[Dbmaj7, DbMA7, Db△7]

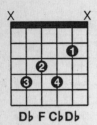

Db F Cb Db

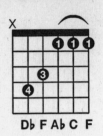

Db F Ab C F

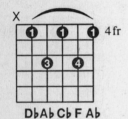

Db Ab Cb F Ab — 4 fr

Db Ab C F Ab — 4 fr

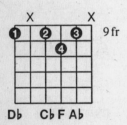

Db Cb F Ab — 9 fr

Db C F Ab — 9 fr

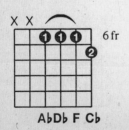

Ab Db F Cb — 6 fr

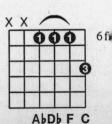

Ab Db F C — 6 fr

Db MINOR SEVENTH
[Dbm7, Dbmi7, Db-7]

Db MINOR MAJOR SEVENTH
[Dbm(maj7), Dbm#7]

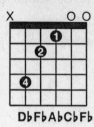

DbFbAbCbFb

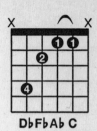

DbFbAb C

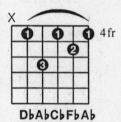

4 fr

DbAbCbFbAb

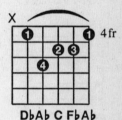

4 fr

DbAb C FbAb

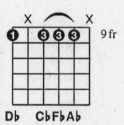

9 fr

Db CbFbAb

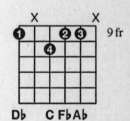

9 fr

Db C FbAb

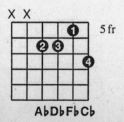

5 fr

AbDbFbCb

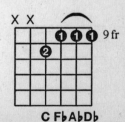

9 fr

C FbAbDb

30

Db MINOR SEVENTH FLATTED FIFTH
[Dbm7b5, Dbmi7b5, Db-7b5, Db∅7]

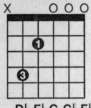

Db Fb G Cb Fb

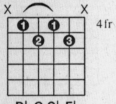

4 fr

Db G Cb Fb

X   X

8 fr

Db   Cb Fb G

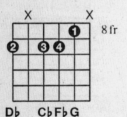

11 fr

Db G Cb Fb

Db DIMINISHED SEVENTH
[Dbdim7, Db°7, Dbdim]

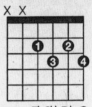

Fb Cbb Db G

X

Db G Cbb Fb G

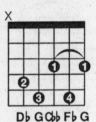

8 fr

Db   Cbb Fb G

X X

8 fr

Cbb Fb G Db

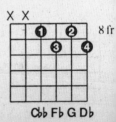

Db SEVENTH SUSPENDED FOURTH
[Db7sus, Db7sus4]

Db SEVENTH SHARPED FIFTH
[Db7#5, Db+7]

DbGbCbDb

Db F A Cb F

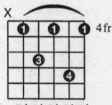

4 fr

DbAbCbGbAb

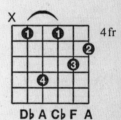

4 fr

Db A Cb F A

9 fr

DbAbCbGbAbDb

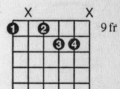

9 fr

Db Cb F A

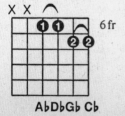

6 fr

AbDbGb Cb

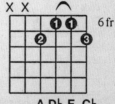

6 fr

A Db F Cb

32

Db NINTH
[Db9]

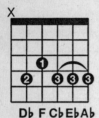

Db F Cb Eb Ab

8 fr

F Cb Eb Ab

9 fr

Db Ab Cb F Ab Eb

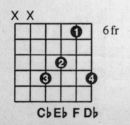

6 fr

Cb Eb F Db

Db MAJOR NINTH
[Dbmaj9, DbMA9, Db△9]

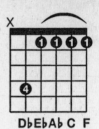

Db Eb Ab C F

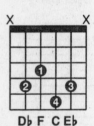

Db F C Eb

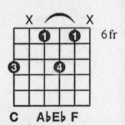

6 fr

C Ab Eb F

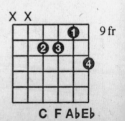

9 fr

C F Ab Eb

Db MINOR NINTH
[Dbm9, Dbmi9, Db-9]

Db ADDED NINTH
[Db(add9), Db(9), Db(add2)]

DbFbCbEbAb

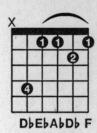

DbEbAbDb F

9 fr

DbAbCbFbAbEb

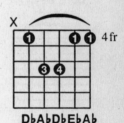

4 fr

DbAbDbEbAb

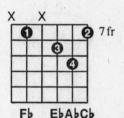

7 fr

Fb EbAbCb

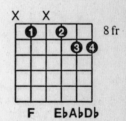

8 fr

F EbAbDb

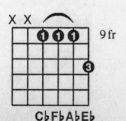

9 fr

CbFbAbEb

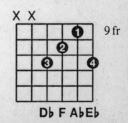

9 fr

Db F AbEb

Db SIX NINE

[Db6/9, Db$^6_9$]

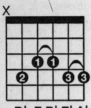

Db F Bb Eb Ab

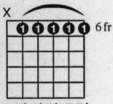

6 fr

Eb Ab Db F Bb

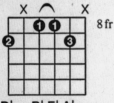

8 fr

Db   Bb Eb Ab

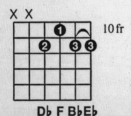

10 fr

Db F Bb Eb

Db SEVENTH SHARPED NINE

[Db7#9]

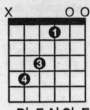

Db F Ab Cb E

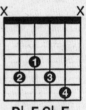

Db F Cb E

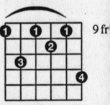

9 fr

Db Ab Cb F Ab E

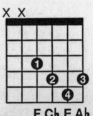

F Cb E Ab

Db SEVENTH FLATTED NINE

[Db7b9]

Db F Cb Ebb

7 fr

F Cb Ebb Ab

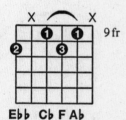

9 fr

Ebb Cb F Ab

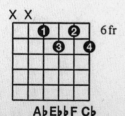

6 fr

Ab Ebb F Cb

Db FIFTH

[Db5, Db(no3)]

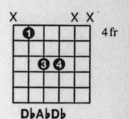

4 fr

Db Ab Db

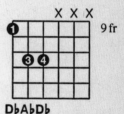

9 fr

Db Ab Db

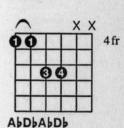

4 fr

Ab Db Ab Db

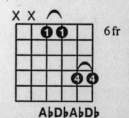

6 fr

Ab Db Ab Db

D CHORDS

D MAJOR
[D]

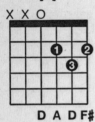

X X O

D A D F#

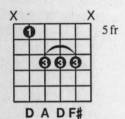

X   X   5 fr

D A D F#

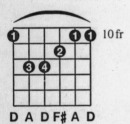

10 fr

D A D F# A D

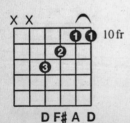

X X   10 fr

D F# A D

D MINOR
[Dm, Dmi, D-]

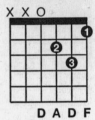

X X O

D A D F

X   5 fr

D A D F A

10

D A D F A D

X X   10

D F A D

D AUGMENTED
[D+, Daug, D(#5)]

D SUSPENDED FOURTH
[Dsus, Dsus4]

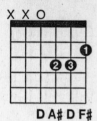

D A# D F#

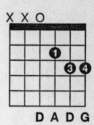

D A D G

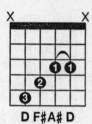

D F#A# D

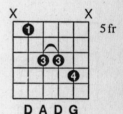

D A D G

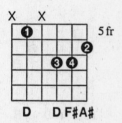

D   D F#A#

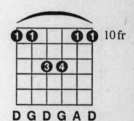

D G D G A D

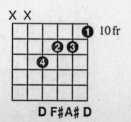

D F#A# D

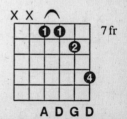

A D G D

D SIXTH
[D6]

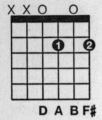

D A B F#

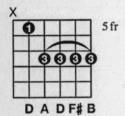

5 fr

D A D F# B

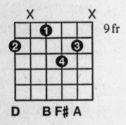

9 fr

D B F# A

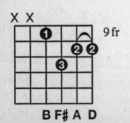

9 fr

B F# A D

D MINOR SIXTH
[Dm6, Dmi6, D-6]

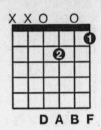

D A B F

D F B D A

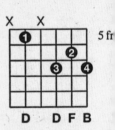

5 fr

D D F B

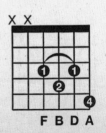

F B D A

D SEVENTH
[D7]

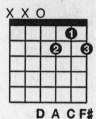

D A C F#

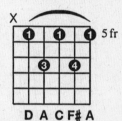

D A C F# A

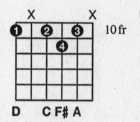

D C F# A

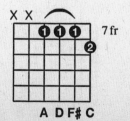

A D F# C

D MAJOR SEVENTH
[Dmaj7, DMA7, D△7]

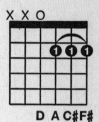

D A C#F#

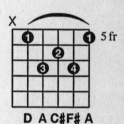

D A C#F# A

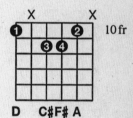

D C#F# A

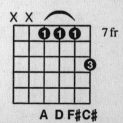

A D F#C#

D MINOR SEVENTH
[Dm7, Dmi7, D-7]

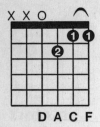

X X O

D A C F

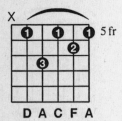

X   5 fr

D A C F A

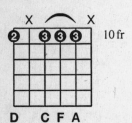

X   X   10 fr

D   C F A

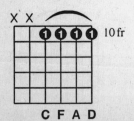

X X   10 fr

C F A D

D MINOR MAJOR SEVENTH
[Dm(maj7), Dm#7]

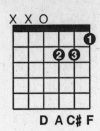

X X O

D A C# F

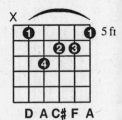

X   5 fr

D A C# F A

X   X   10 f

D   C# F A

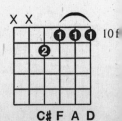

X X   10 f

C# F A D

41

D MINOR SEVENTH FLATTED FIFTH

[Dm7♭5, Dmi7♭5, D-7♭5, D♯7]

D DIMINISHED SEVENTH

[Ddim7, D°7, Ddim]

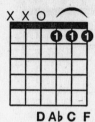

D A♭ C F

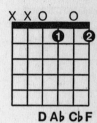

D A♭ C♭ F

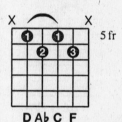

D A♭ C F

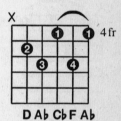

D A♭ C♭ F A♭

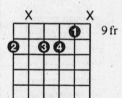

D C F A♭

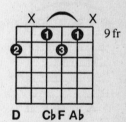

D C♭ F A♭

F C D A♭

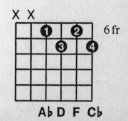

A♭ D F C♭

D SEVENTH SUSPENDED FOURTH

[D7sus, D7sus4]

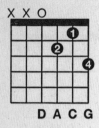

D A C G

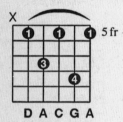

D A C G A

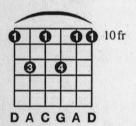

D A C G A D

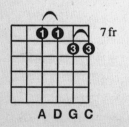

A D G C

D SEVENTH SHARPED FIFTH

[D7#5, D+7]

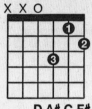

D A# C F#

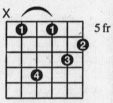

D A# C F# A#

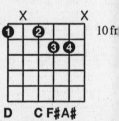

D C F# A#

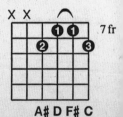

A# D F# C

D NINTH
[D9]

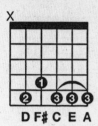

D F# C E A

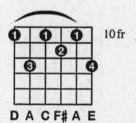

F# C E A

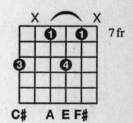

D A C F# A E

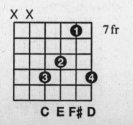

C E F# D

D MAJOR NINTH
[Dmaj9, DMA9, DΔ9]

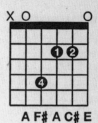

A F# A C# E

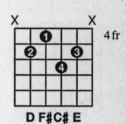

D F# C# E

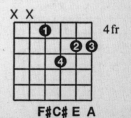

C# A E F#

F# C# E A

D MINOR NINTH
[Dm9, Dmi9, D-9]

D ADDED NINTH
[D(add9), D(9), D(add2)]

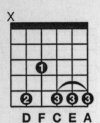

D F C E A

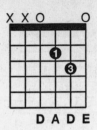

D A D E

10 fr

D A C F A E

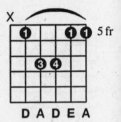

5 fr

D A D E A

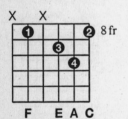

8 fr

F E A C

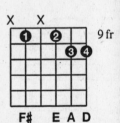

9 fr

F# E A D

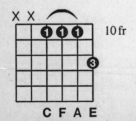

10 fr

C F A E

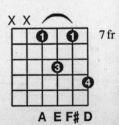

7 fr

A E F# D

45

D SIX NINE

[D6/9, D$_9^6$]

X X O

D B E F#

X

D F# B E A

X   X   9 fr

D   B E A

X X   7 fr

B E F# D

D SEVENTH SHARPED NINTH

[D7#9]

X   X   4 fr

D F# C E#

X   7 fr

E# A D F# C

10 fr

D A C F# A E#

X X   11 fr

D F# C E#

D SEVENTH FLATTED NINTH

[D7♭9]

X X

Eb A C F#

X X

D F# C Eb

X X 10 fr

Eb C F# A

X X 7 fr

A Eb F# C

D FIFTH

[D5, D(no3)]

X O O

A D A D A

X X X 5 fr

D A D

X X X 10 fr

D A D

X X 7 fr

A D A D

E♭ CHORDS

E♭ and D♯ are enharmonically equivalent. For the sake of convenience, all chords have been notated as E♭ chords.

E♭ MAJOR
[E♭]

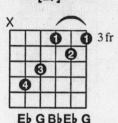

E♭ G B♭ E♭ G

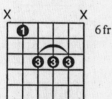

E♭ B♭ E♭ G

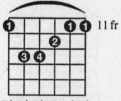

E♭ B♭ E♭ G B♭ E♭

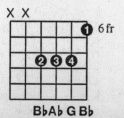

B♭ A♭ G B♭

E♭ MINOR
[E♭m, E♭MI, E♭-]

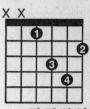

E♭ B♭ E♭ G♭

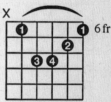

E♭ B♭ E♭ G♭ B♭

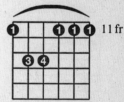

E♭ B♭ E♭ G♭ B♭ E♭

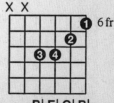

B♭ E♭ G♭ B♭

Eb AUGMENTED
[Eb+, Ebaug, Eb(#5)]

Eb SUSPENDED FOURTH
[Ebsus, Ebsus4]

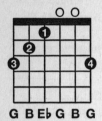

G B Eb G B G

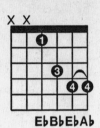

Eb Bb Eb Ab

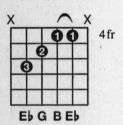

4 fr

Eb G B Eb

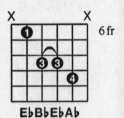

6 fr

Eb Bb Eb Ab

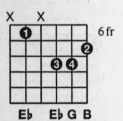

6 fr

Eb   Eb G B

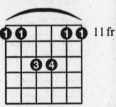

11 fr

Eb Ab Eb Ab Bb Eb

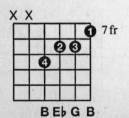

7 fr

B Eb G B

8 fr

Bb Eb Ab Eb

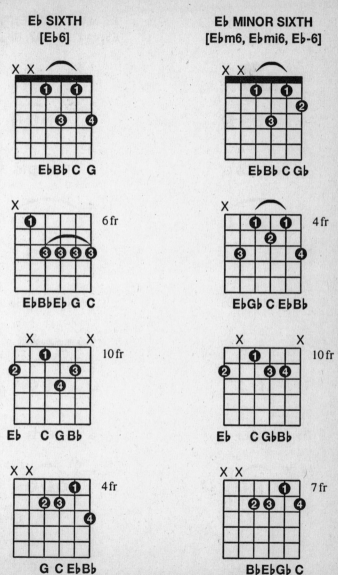

Eb SIXTH
[Eb6]

Eb MINOR SIXTH
[Ebm6, Ebmi6, Eb-6]

EbBb C G

EbBb C Gb

6 fr
EbBbEb G C

4 fr
EbGb C EbBb

10 fr
Eb C G Bb

10 fr
Eb C Gb Bb

4 fr
G C EbBb

7 fr
BbEbGb C

Eb SEVENTH
[Eb7]

Eb MAJOR SEVENTH
[Ebmaj7, EbMA7, Eb△7]

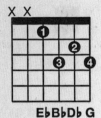

EbBbDb G

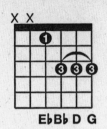

EbBb D G

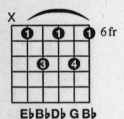

EbBbDb G Bb

6 fr

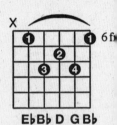

EbBb D G Bb

6 fr

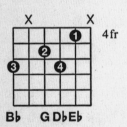

4 fr

Bb G DbEb

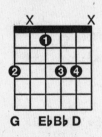

4 fr

G EbBb D

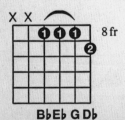

8 fr

BbEb G Db

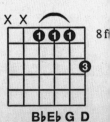

8 fr

BbEb G D

Eb MINOR SEVENTH
[Ebm7, Ebmi7, Eb-7]

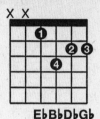

EbBbDbGb

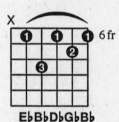

EbBbDbGbBb

Gb   EbBbDb

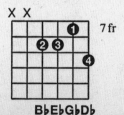

BbEbGbDb

Eb MINOR MAJOR SEVENTH
[Ebm(maj7), Ebm#7]

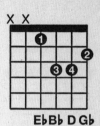

EbBb D Gb

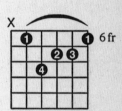

EbBb D GbBb

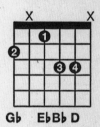

Gb   EbBb D

D GbBbEb

52

Eb MINOR SEVENTH FLATTED FIFTH
[Ebm7b5, Ebmi7b5, Eb-7b5, Eb∅7]

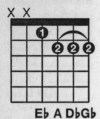

Eb A Db Gb

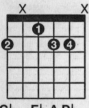

Eb A Db Gb   6 fr

Gb Eb A Db

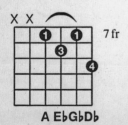

A Eb Gb Db   7 fr

Eb DIMINISHED SEVENTH
[Ebdim7, Eb°7, Ebdim]

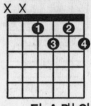

Eb A Dbb Gb

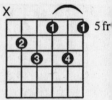

Eb A Dbb Gb A   5 fr

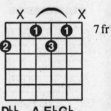

Dbb A Eb Gb   7 fr

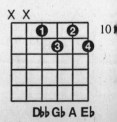

Dbb Gb A Eb   10 fr

Eb SEVENTH SUSPENDED FOURTH
[Eb7sus, Eb7sus4]

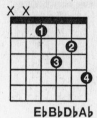

EbBbDbAb

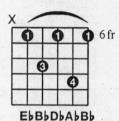

EbBbDbAbBb

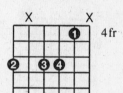

Bb AbDbEb

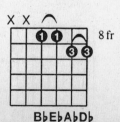

BbEbAbDb

Eb SEVENTH SHARPED FIFTH
[Eb7#5, Eb+7]

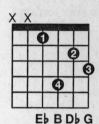

Eb B Db G

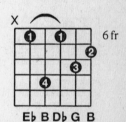

Eb B Db G B

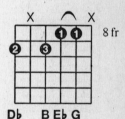

Db B Eb G

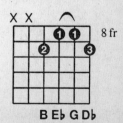

B Eb G Db

Eb NINTH
[Eb9]

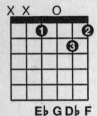

Eb G Db F

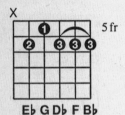

Eb G Db F Bb

5 fr

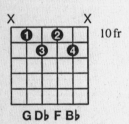

G Db F Bb

10 fr

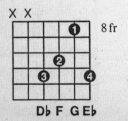

Db F G Eb

8 fr

Eb MAJOR NINTH
[Ebmaj9, EbMA9, Eb△9]

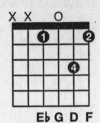

Eb G D F

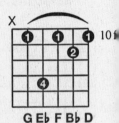

G Eb F Bb D

10 fr

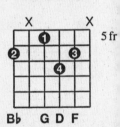

Bb G D F

5 fr

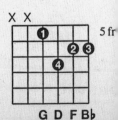

G D F Bb

5 fr

Eb MINOR NINTH
[Ebm9, Ebmi9, Eb-9]

Eb ADDED NINTH
[Eb(add9), Eb(9), Eb(add2)]

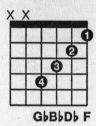

GbBbDb F

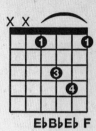

EbBbEb F

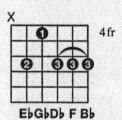

4 fr

EbGbDb F Bb

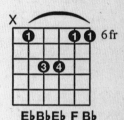

6 fr

EbBbEb F Bb

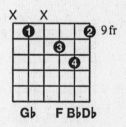

9 fr

Gb   F BbDb

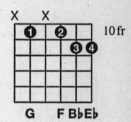

10 fr

G   F BbEb

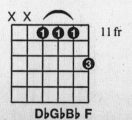

11 fr

DbGbBb F

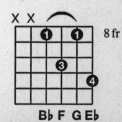

8 fr

Bb F G Eb

Eb SIX NINE

[Eb6/9, Eb⁶⁄₉]

X   O

Bb Eb G C F

5 fr

Eb G C F Bb

10 fr

Eb   C F Bb

6 fr

Bb Eb F C

Eb SEVENTH SHARPED NINE

[Eb7#9]

X X   O

Eb G Db F#

5 fr

Eb G Db F#

8 fr

F# Bb Eb G Db

5 fr

G Db F# Bb

Eb SEVENTH FLATTED NINE

[Eb7b9]

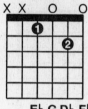

Eb G Db Fb

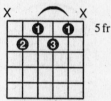

5 fr

Eb F Db Fb

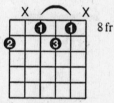

8 fr

Db   Bb Fb G

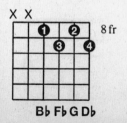

8 fr

Bb Fb G Db

Eb FIFTH

[Eb5, Eb(no3)]

Bb Eb Bb Eb

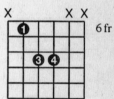

6 fr

Eb Bb Eb

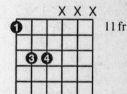

11 fr

Eb Bb Eb

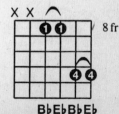

8 fr

Bb Eb Bb Eb

E CHORDS

E MAJOR
[E]

E B E G# B E

E B E G#

E G# B E G#

B E G# E

E MINOR
[Em, Emi, E-]

E B E G B E

E B E G B

E B E B E G

G B E G

E AUGMENTED
[E+, Eaug, E(#5)]

E SUSPENDED FOURTH
[Esus, Esus4]

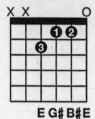

E G# B# E

E B E A B E

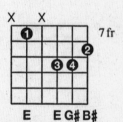

E G# B# E

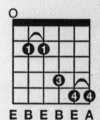

E B E A

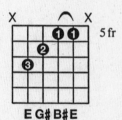

E   E G# B#

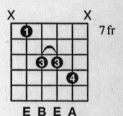

E B E B E A

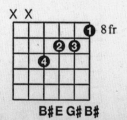

B# E G# B#

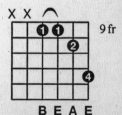

B E A E

60

E SIXTH
[E6]

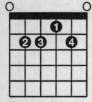

E B E G#C# E

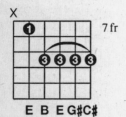

E B E G#C#

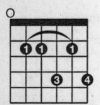

E B E B C#G#

G#C# E B

E MINOR SIXTH
[Em6, Emi6, E-6]

E B E G C# E

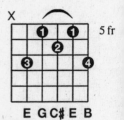

E G C# E B

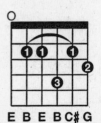

E B E B C#G

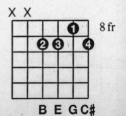

B E G C#

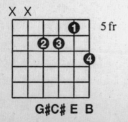

E SEVENTH
[E7]

E B D G# B E

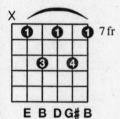

E B D G# B

X

X
5 fr

B   G# D E

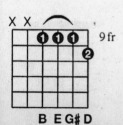

B E G# D

E MAJOR SEVENTH
[Emaj7, EMA7, EΔ7]

E B D#G# B E

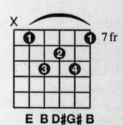

E B D#G# B

G#   E B D#

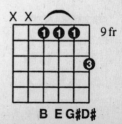

B E G#D#

E MINOR SEVENTH
[Em7, Emi7, E-7]

E MINOR MAJOR SEVENTH
[Em(maj7), Em#7]

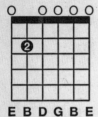

E B D G B E

E BD# G B E

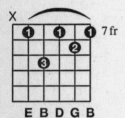

E B D G B

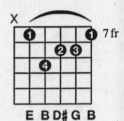

E BD# G B

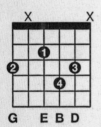

G E B D

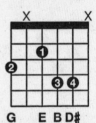

G E BD#

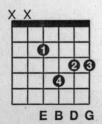

E B D G

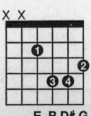

E BD# G

E MINOR SEVENTH FLATTED FIFTH

[Em7♭5, Emi7♭5, E-7♭5, E♯7]

E B♭ E G D E

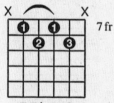

7 fr

E B♭ D G

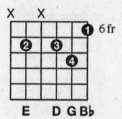

6 fr

E D G B♭

E B♭ D G

E DIMINISHED SEVENTH

[Edim7, E°7, Edim]

E B♭ E G D♭ E

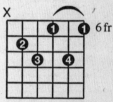

6 fr

E B♭ D♭ G B♭

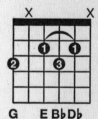

G E B♭ D♭

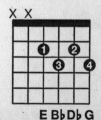

E B♭ D♭ G

E SEVENTH SUSPENDED FOURTH

[E7sus, E7sus4]

E B D A B E

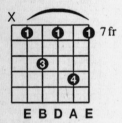

E B D A E

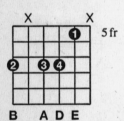

B   A D E

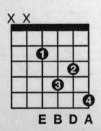

E B D A

E SEVENTH SHARPED FIFTH

[E7#5, E+7]

E B# E G# D E

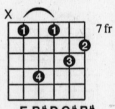

E B# D G# B#

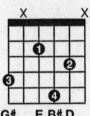

G#   E B# D

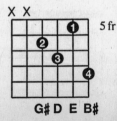

G# D E B#

E NINTH
[E9]

E MAJOR NINTH
[Emaj9, EMA9, E△9]

E B D G# B F#

E B F# B D#G#

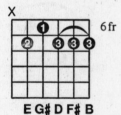

6 fr

E G# D F# B

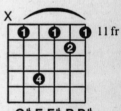

11 fr

G# E F# B D#

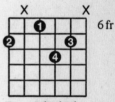

E E G# D F#

B G#D#F#

6 fr

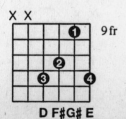

9 fr

D F#G# E

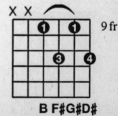

9 fr

B F#G#D#

E MINOR NINTH
[Em9, Emi9, E-9]

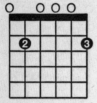

E B D G B F#

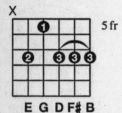

5 fr

E G D F# B

10 fr

G   F# B D

X X O O O

D G B F#

E ADDED NINTH
[E(add9), E(9), E(add2)]

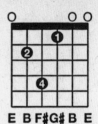

E B F#G# B E

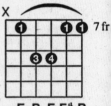

7 fr

E B E F# B

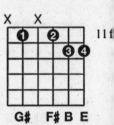

11 f

G#   F# B E

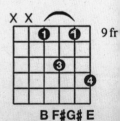

9 fr

B F#G# E

67

E SIX NINE

[E6/9, E⁶₉]

E B E G#C#F#

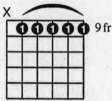

F# B E G#C# — 9 fr

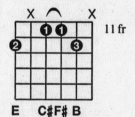

E C#F# B — 11 fr

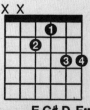

E G#C#F#

E SEVENTH SHARPED NINTH

[E7#9]

E B D G#B F✕

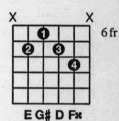

E G# D F✕ — 6 fr

G# D F✕B E — 11 fr

E G# D F✕

E SEVENTH FLATTED NINTH

[E7♭9]

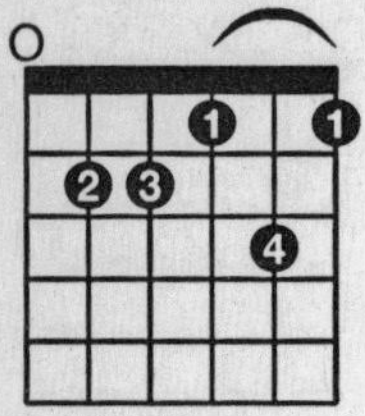

E B E G# D F

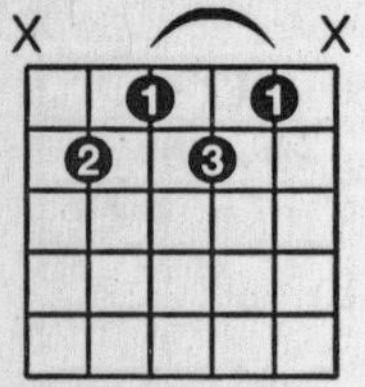

6 fr

E G# D F

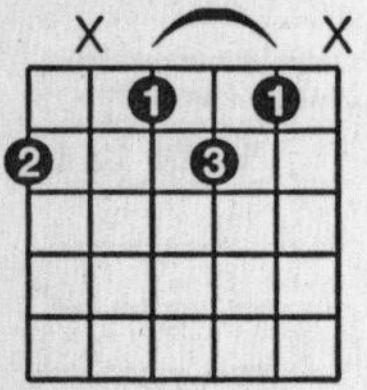

9 fr

D B F G#

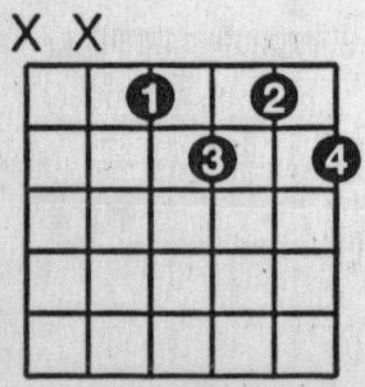

6 fr

G# D F B

E FIFTH

[E5, E(no3)]

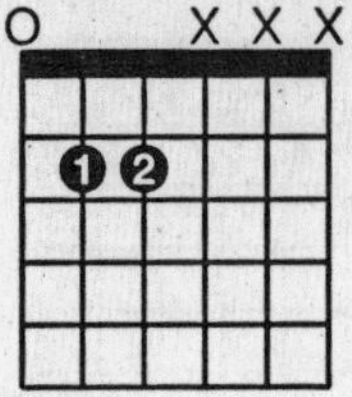

E B E

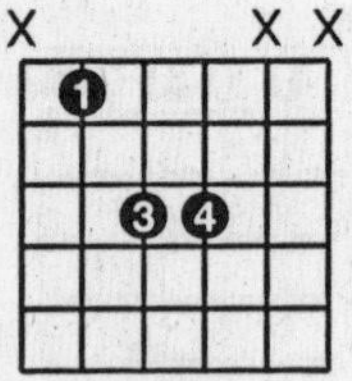

7 fr

E B E

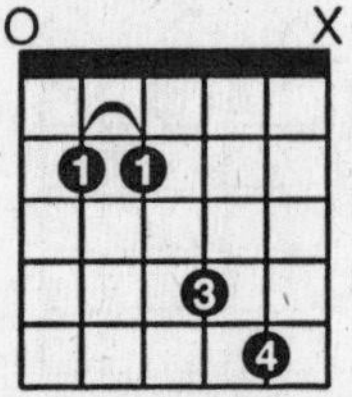

E B E B E

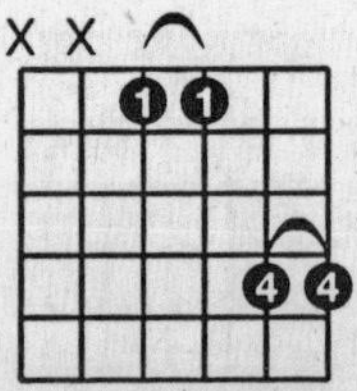

9 fr

B E B E

F CHORDS

F MAJOR
[F]

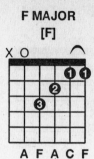

A F A C F

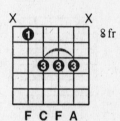

8 fr

F C F A

F C F A C F

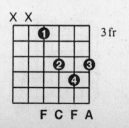

3 fr

F C F A

F MINOR
[Fm, Fmi, F-]

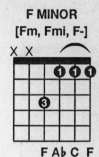

F Ab C F

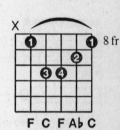

8 fr

F C F Ab C

F C F Ab C F

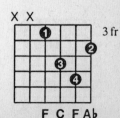

3 fr

F C F Ab

F AUGMENTED
[F+, Faug, F(#5)]

F SUSPENDED FOURTH
[Fsus, Fsus4]

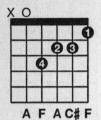

A F A C# F

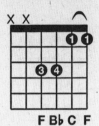

F Bb C F

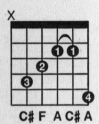

C# F A C# A

8 fr

F C F Bb

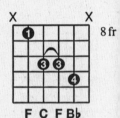

8 fr

F   F A C#

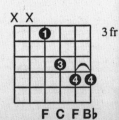

F Bb F Bb C F

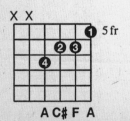

5 fr

A C# F A

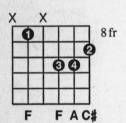

3 fr

F C F Bb

F SIXTH
[F6]

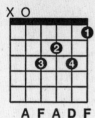

A F A D F

8 fr

F C F A D

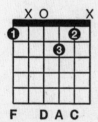

F D A C

F C D A

F MINOR SIXTH
[Fm6, Fmi6, F-6]

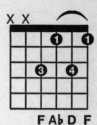

F A♭ D F

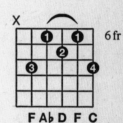

6 fr

F A♭ D F C

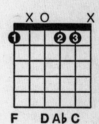

F D A♭ C

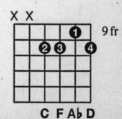

9 fr

C F A♭ D

72

F SEVENTH
[F7]

A E♭ A C F

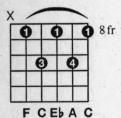

F C E♭ A C · 8 fr

C A E♭ F · 6 fr

F C E♭ A

F MAJOR SEVENTH
[Fmaj7, FMA7, F△7]

A F A C E

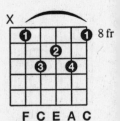

F C E A C · 8 fr

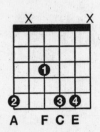

A F C E

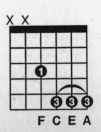

F C E A

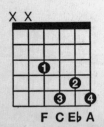

F MINOR SEVENTH
[Fm7, Fmi7, F-7]

F MINOR MAJOR SEVENTH
[Fm(maj7), Fm#7]

F C Eb Bb C F

F C E Ab C F

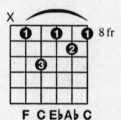

F C Eb Ab C

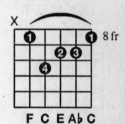

F C E Ab C

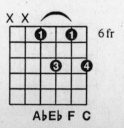

C   Ab Eb F

AbEb F C

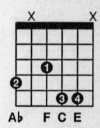

Ab   F C E

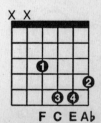

F C E Ab

F MINOR SEVENTH FLATTED FIFTH

[Fm7b5, Fmi7b5, F-7b5, F#7]

F DIMINISHED SEVENTH

[Fdim7, F°7, Fdim]

Cb F AbEb F

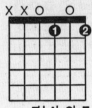

EbbAb Cb F

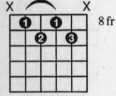

F CbEbAb

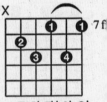

F Cb EbbAb Cb

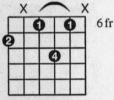

Cb AbEb F

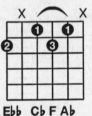

Ebb Cb F Ab

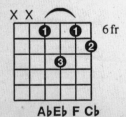

AbEb F Cb

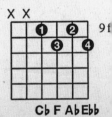

Cb F AbEbb

F SEVENTH SUSPENDED FOURTH

[F7sus, F7sus4]

F C Eb Bb C F

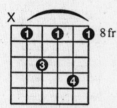

F C Eb Bb C

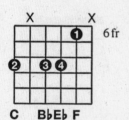

C   Bb Eb F

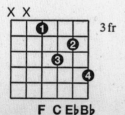

F C Eb Bb

F SEVENTH SHARPED FIFTH

[F7#5, F+7]

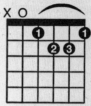

A Eb A C# F

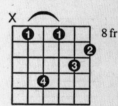

F C#Eb A C#

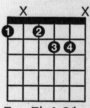

F   Eb A C#

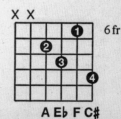

A Eb F C#

F NINTH
[F9]

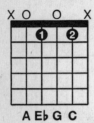

A Eb G C

F A Eb G C

7 fr

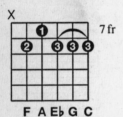

F C Eb A C G

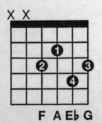

F A Eb G

F MAJOR NINTH
[FMaj9, FMA9, FΔ9]

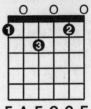

F A E G C E

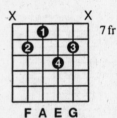

F A E G

7 fr

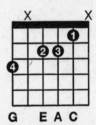

G E A C

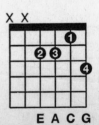

E A C G

F MINOR NINTH
[Fm9, Fmi9, F-9]

F C Eb Ab C G

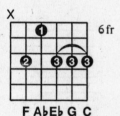

6 fr

F Ab Eb G C

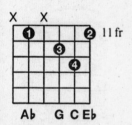

11 fr

Ab G C Eb

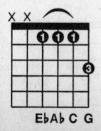

Eb Ab C G

F ADDED NINTH
[F(add9), F(9), F(add2)]

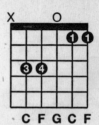

C F G C F

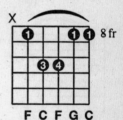

8 fr

F C F G C

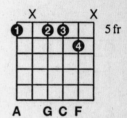

5 fr

A G C F

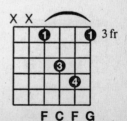

3 fr

F C F G

F SIX NINE

[F6/9, F$_9^6$]

F SEVENTH SHARPED NINTH

[F7#9]

F A D G C F

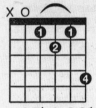

A E♭ A C G#

10 fr

G C F A D

7 fr

F A E♭ G#

7 fr

C A D G

F C E♭ A C G#

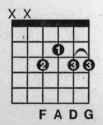

F A D G

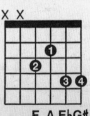

F A E♭ G#

79

F SEVENTH FLATTED NINTH

[F7b9]

A Eb A C Gb

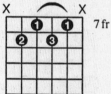
7 fr

F A Eb Gb

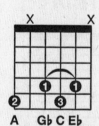

A Gb C Eb

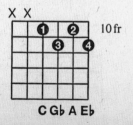
10 fr

C Gb A Eb

F FIFTH

[F5, F(no3)]

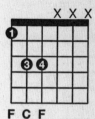

F C F

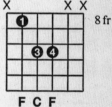
8 fr

F C F

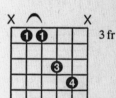
3 fr

C F C F

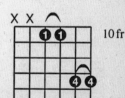
10 fr

C F C F

F♯ CHORDS

F♯ and G♭ are enharmonically equivalent. For the sake of convenience,
all chords have been notated as F♯ chords.

F♯ MAJOR
[F♯]

F♯ MINOR
[F♯m, F♯mi, F♯-]

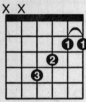

F♯A♯C♯F♯

F♯ A C♯F♯

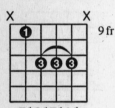

9 fr

F♯C♯F♯A♯

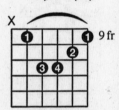

9 fr

F♯C♯F♯ A C♯

F♯C♯F♯A♯C♯F♯

F♯C♯F♯ A C♯F♯

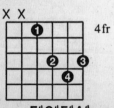

4 fr

F♯C♯F♯A♯

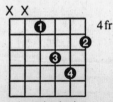

4 fr

F♯C♯F♯ A

F# AUGMENTED
[F#+, F#aug, F#(#5)]

F# SUSPENDED FOURTH
[F#sus, F#sus4]

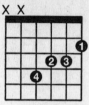

F#A#C✕F#

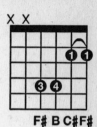

F# B C#F#

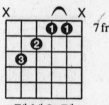

F#A#C✕F#

F#C#F# B

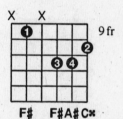

F#   F#A#C✕

F# B F# B C#F#

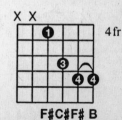

A#C✕F#A#

F#C#F# B

82

F# SIXTH
[F#6]

F# MINOR SIXTH
[F#m6, F#mi6, F#-6]

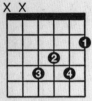

F#A#D#F#

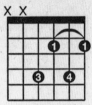

F# A D#F#

F#C#F#A#D#

F#C#F# A D#F#

F# D#A#C#

F# D# A C#

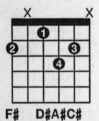

F#C#D#A#

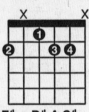

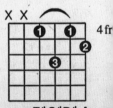

F#C#D# A

F# SEVENTH
[F#7]

E A#C#F#

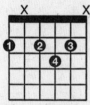

9 fr

F#C# E A#C#

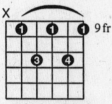

F#   E A#C#

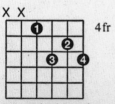

4 fr

F#C# E A#

F# MAJOR SEVENTH
[F#maj7, F#MA7, F#△7]

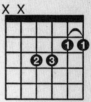

E#A#C#F#

9 fr

F#C#E#A#C#

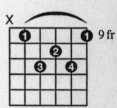

F#   E#A#C#

4 fr

F#C#E#A#

F# MINOR SEVENTH
[F#m7, F#mi7, F#-7]

F# MINOR MAJOR SEVEN
[F#m(maj7), F#m#7]

E A C#F#

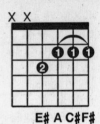

E# A C#F#

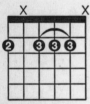

F#C# E A C#

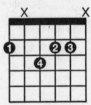

F#C#E# A C#

F# E A C#

F# E# A C#

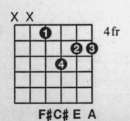

F#C# E A

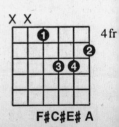

F#C#E# A

F# MINOR SEVENTH FLATTED FIFTH

[F#m7b5, F#mi7b5, F#-7b5, F#°7]

X X

E A C F#

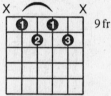

X X   9 fr

F# C E A

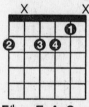

X X

F# E A C

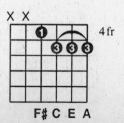

X X   4 fr

F# C E A

F# DIMINISHED SEVENTH

[F#dim7, F#°7, F#dim]

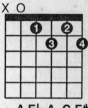

X O

A Eb A C F#

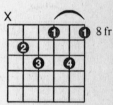

X   8 fr

F# C Eb A C

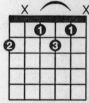

X X

F# Eb A C

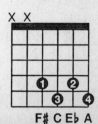

X X

F# C Eb A

86

F# SEVENTH SUSPENDED FOURTH
[F#7sus, F#7sus4]

E B C#F#

F#C# E B C# 9 fr

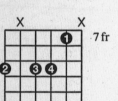

C#   B E F# 7 fr

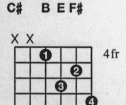

F#C# E B 4 fr

F# SEVENTH SHARPED FIFTH
[F#7#5, F#+7]

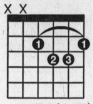

E A#C✕F#

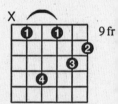

F#C✕ E A#C✕ 9 fr

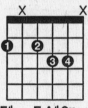

F#   E A#C✕

C✕F#A# E 11 f

F# NINTH
[F#9]

A# E G#C#

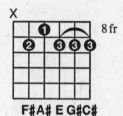

8 fr

F#A# E G#C#

F#C# E A#C#G#

X X

F#A# E G#

F# MAJOR NINTH
[F#maj9, F#MA9, F#△9]

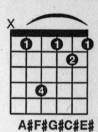

A#F#G#C#E#

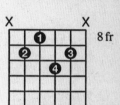

8 fr

F#A#E#G#

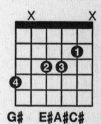

G# E#A#C#

X X

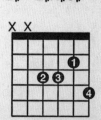

E#A#C#G#

F# MINOR NINTH
[F#m9, F#mi9, F#-9]

F# ADDED NINTH
[F#(add9), F#(9), F#(add2

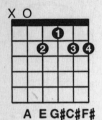

A E G#C#F#

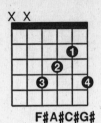

F#A#C#G#

7 fr

F# A E G#C#

9 fr

F#C#F#G#C#

F#C# E A C#G#

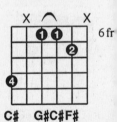

6 fr

C# G#C#F#

E A C#G#

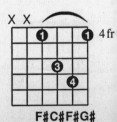

4 fr

F#C#F#G#

89

F# SIX NINE

[F#6/9, F#$^6_9$]

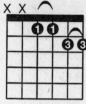

D#G#C#F#

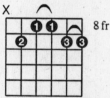

8 fr

F#A#D#G#C#

F#   D#G#C#

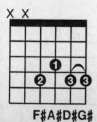

F#A#D#G#

F# SEVENTH SHARPED NINE

[F#7#9]

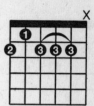

F#A# E G×C#

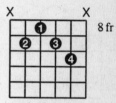

8 fr

F#A# E G×

F#C# E A#C#G×

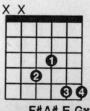

F#A# E G×

F# SEVENTH FLATTED NINE

[F#7b9]

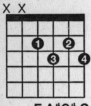

E A# C# G

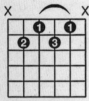 8 fr

F# A# E G

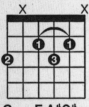

G   E A# C#

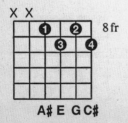 8 fr

A# E G C#

F# FIFTH

[F#5, F#(no3)]

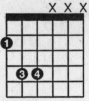

F# C# F#

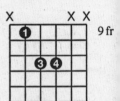 9 fr

F# C# F#

 4 fr

C# F# C# F#

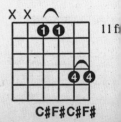 11 fr

C# F# C# F#

G CHORDS

G MAJOR
[G]

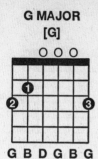

G B D G B G

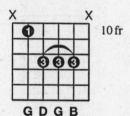

10 fr

G D G B

G D G B D G

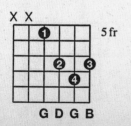

5 fr

G D G B

G MINOR
[Gm, Gmi, G-]

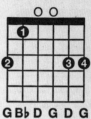

G Bb D G D G

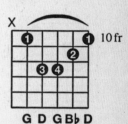

10 fr

G D G Bb D

G D G Bb D G

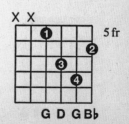

5 fr

G D G Bb

G AUGMENTED
[G+, Gaug, G(#5)]

G SUSPENDED FOURTH
[Gsus, Gsus4]

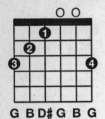

G B D# G B G

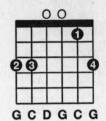

G C D G C G

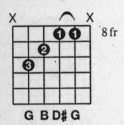

8 fr

G B D# G

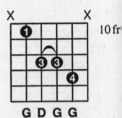

10 fr

G D G G

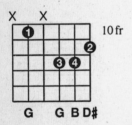

10 fr

G   G B D#

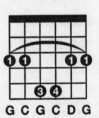

G C G C D G

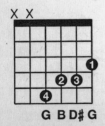

G B D# G

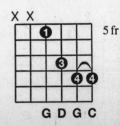

5 fr

G D G C

G SIXTH
[G6]

G MINOR SIXTH
[Gm6, Gmi6, G-6]

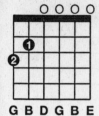

G B D G B E

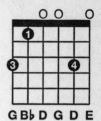

G Bb D G D E

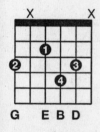

10 fr

G D G B E

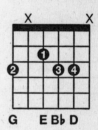

G D G Bb E G

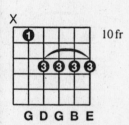

G E B D

G E Bb D

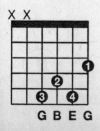

G B E G

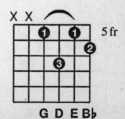

5 fr

G D E Bb

G SEVENTH
[G7]

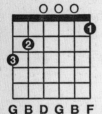

G B D G B F

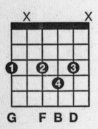

G D F B D — 10 fr

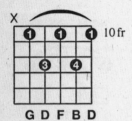

G F B D

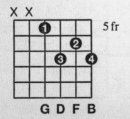

G D F B — 5 fr

G MAJOR SEVENTH
[Gmaj7, GMA7, G△7]

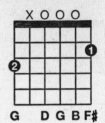

G D G B F#

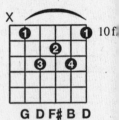

G D F# B D — 10 fr

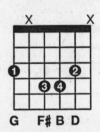

G F# B D

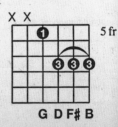

G D F# B — 5 fr

G MINOR SEVENTH
[Gm7, GMI7, G-7]

G MINOR MAJOR SEVENTH
[Gm(maj7), Gm#7]

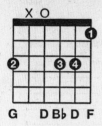

G   D B♭ D F

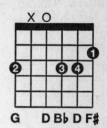

G   D B♭ D F#

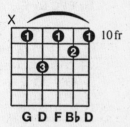

G D F B♭ D

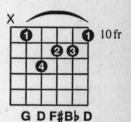

G D F#B♭ D

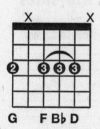

G   F B♭ D

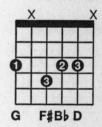

G   F#B♭ D

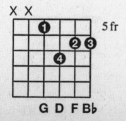

G D F B♭

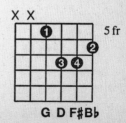

G D F#B♭

G MINOR SEVENTH FLATTED FIFTH

[Gm7b5, Gmi7b5, G-7b5, G♯7]

F Bb Db G

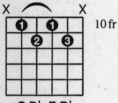

10 fr

G Db F Bb

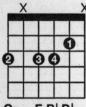

G F Bb Db

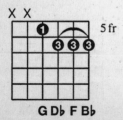

5 fr

G Db F Bb

G DIMINISHED SEVENTH

[Gdim7, G°7, Gdim]

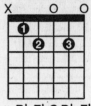

Bb Fb G Db Fb

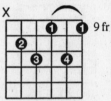

9 fr

G Db Fb Bb Db

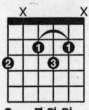

G Fb Bb Db

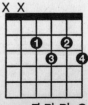

Fb Bb Db G

G SEVENTH SUSPENDED FOURTH

[G7sus, G7sus4]

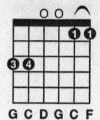

G C D G C F

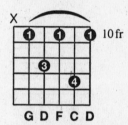

G D F C D

G D F C D G

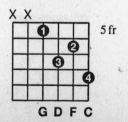

G D F C

G SEVENTH SHARPED FIFTH

[G7#5, G+7]

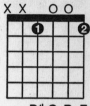

D# G B F

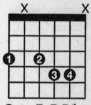

G D# F B D#

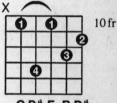

G F B D#

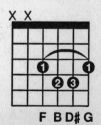

F B D# G

G NINTH
[G9]

G MAJOR NINTH
[Gmaj9, GMA9, G△9]

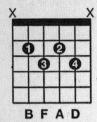

X   X

B F A D

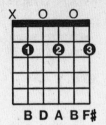

X   O   O

B D A B F#

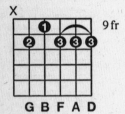

9 fr

G B F A D

9 fr

G B F# A

G D F B D A

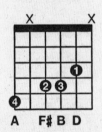

A   F# B D

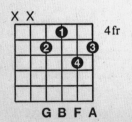

X X   4 fr

G B F A

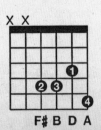

X X

F# B D A

G MINOR NINTH
[Gm9, Gmi9, G-9]

G ADDED NINTH
[G(add9), G(9), G(add2)]

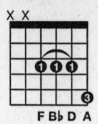

F Bb D A

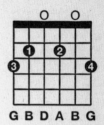

G B D A B G

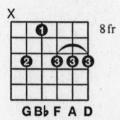

8 fr

G Bb F A D

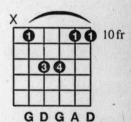

10 fr

G D G A D

G D F Bb D A

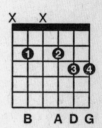

B A D G

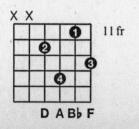

11 fr

D A Bb F

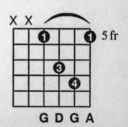

5 fr

G D G A

G SIX NINE
[G6/9, G9^6]

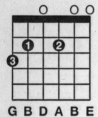

G B D A B E

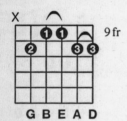

9 fr

G B E A D

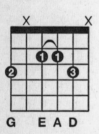

G E A D

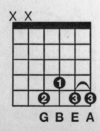

G B E A

G SEVENTH SHARPED NINE
[G7#9]

G B F A# D

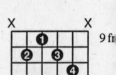

9 fr

G B F A#

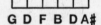

3 fr

G D F B D A#

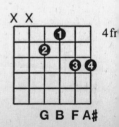

4 fr

G B F A#

G SEVENTH FLATTED NINTH

[G7]

G B F G B Ab

9 fr

G B F Ab

X F B D Ab

Ab F B D

F B D Ab

G FIFTH

[G5, G(no3)]

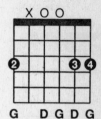

G D G D G

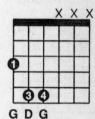

G D G

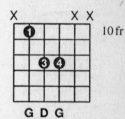

10 fr

G D G

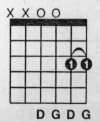

D G D G

Ab CHORDS

Ab and G# are enharmonically equivalent. For the sake of convenience, all chords have been notated as Ab chords.

Ab MAJOR
[Ab]

EbAb C Ab

AbEbAb C — 11 fr

AbEbAb C EbAb — 4 fr

AbEbAb C — 6 fr

Ab MINOR
[Abm, Abmi, Ab-]

CbEbAb Cb

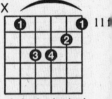

AbEbAbCbEb — 11 fr

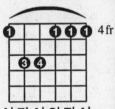

AbEbAbCbEbAb — 4 fr

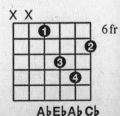

AbEbAb Cb — 6 fr

Ab AUGMENTED
[Ab+, Abaug, Ab(#5)]

Ab SUSPENDED FOURTH
[Absus, Absus4]

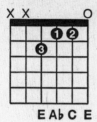

E Ab C E

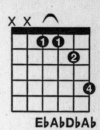

Eb Ab Db Ab

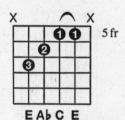

E Ab C E   5 fr

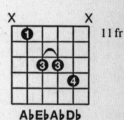

Ab Eb Ab Db   11 fr

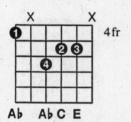

Ab   Ab C E   4 fr

Ab Db Ab Db Eb Ab   4 fr

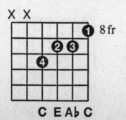

C E Ab C   8 fr

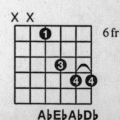

Ab Eb Ab Db   6 fr

Ab SIXTH
[Ab6]

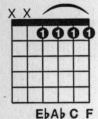

EbAb C F

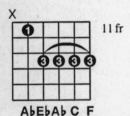

11 fr

AbEbAb C F

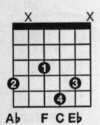

Ab F C Eb

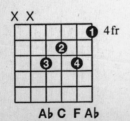

4 fr

Ab C F Ab

Ab MINOR SIXTH
[Abm6, Abmi6, Ab-6]

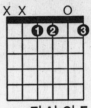

EbAb Cb F

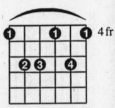

4 fr

AbEbAb Cb F Ab

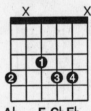

Ab F Cb Eb

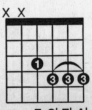

F CbEb Ab

Ab SEVENTH
[Ab7]

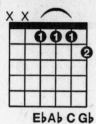

EbAb C Gb

AbEbGb C Eb

11 fr

Ab Gb C Eb

AbEbGb C

6 fr

Ab MAJOR SEVENTH
[Abmaj7, AbMA7, Ab△7]

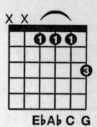

EbAb C G

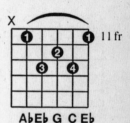

AbEb G C Eb

11 fr

Ab G C Eb

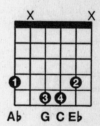

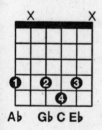

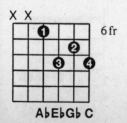

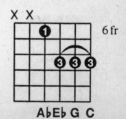

AbEb G C

6 fr

Ab MINOR SEVENTH
[Abm7, Abmi7, Ab-7]

Ab MINOR MAJOR SEVENTH
[Abm(maj7), Abm#7]

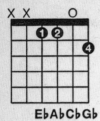

EbAbCbGb

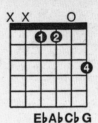

EbAbCb G

AbEbGbCbEb

AbEb G CbEb

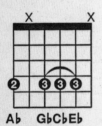

Ab GbCbEb

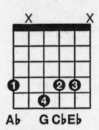

Ab G CbEb

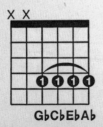

GbCbEbAb

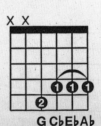

G CbEbAb

Ab MINOR SEVENTH FLATTED FIFTH

[Abm7b5, Abmi7b5, Ab-7b5, Ab♯7]

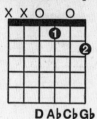

D Ab Cb Gb

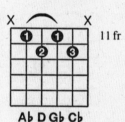

Ab D Gb Cb

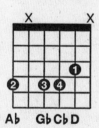

Ab Gb Cb D

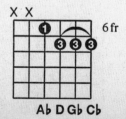

Ab D Gb Cb

Ab DIMINISHED SEVENTH

[Abdim7, Ab°7, Abdim]

D Ab Cb Gbb

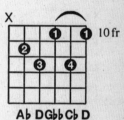

Ab DGbb Cb D

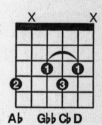

Ab Gbb Cb D

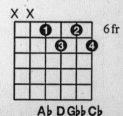

Ab D Gbb Cb

Ab SEVENTH SUSPENDED FOURTH
[Ab7sus, Ab7sus4]

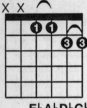

EbAbDbGb

AbEbGbDbEb 11 fr

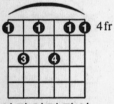

AbEbGbDbEbAb 4 fr

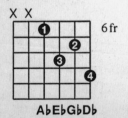

AbEbGbDb 6 fr

Ab SEVENTH SHARPED FIFTH
[Ab7#5, Ab+7]

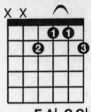

E Ab C Gb

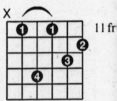

Ab E Gb C E 11 fr

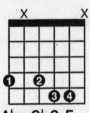

Ab Gb C E

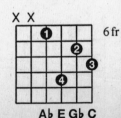

Ab E Gb C 6 fr

Ab NINTH
[Ab9]

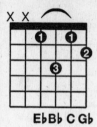

EbBb C Gb

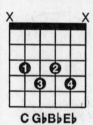

C GbBbEb

AbEbGb C EbBb

4 fr

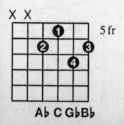

Ab C GbBb

5 fr

Ab MAJOR NINTH
[Abmaj9, AbMA9, AbΔ9]

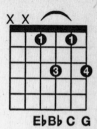

EbBb C G

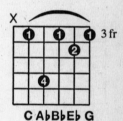

C AbBbEb G

3 fr

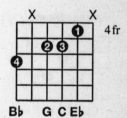

Bb G C Eb

4 fr

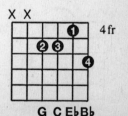

G C EbBb

4 fr

Ab MINOR NINTH
[Abm9, AbMI9, Ab-9]

Ab ADDED NINTH
[Ab(add9), Ab(9), Ab(add2

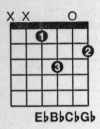

EbBbCbGb

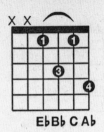

EbBb C Ab

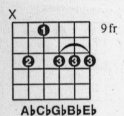

AbCbGbBbEb

AbEbAbBbEb

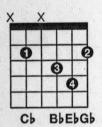

Cb BbEbGb

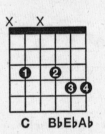

C BbEbAb

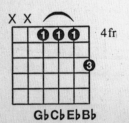

GbCbEbBb

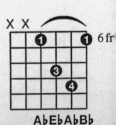

AbEbAbBb

Ab SIX NINE

[Ab6/9, Ab6/9]

Bb Eb Ab C F

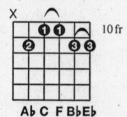

Ab C F Bb Eb

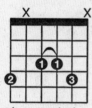

Ab F Bb Eb

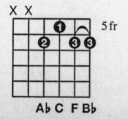

Ab C F Bb

Ab SEVENTH SHARPED NINE

[Ab7#9]

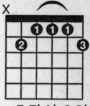

B Eb Ab C Gb

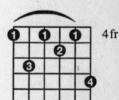

Ab C Gb B

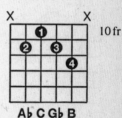

Ab Eb Gb C Eb B

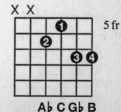

Ab C Gb B

Ab SEVENTH FLATTED NINE

[Ab7b9]

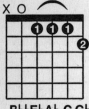

BbbEbAb C Gb

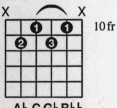

10 fr

Ab C Gb Bbb

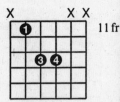

Bbb Gb C Eb

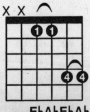

Gb C Eb Bbb

Ab FIFTH

[Ab5, Ab(no3)]

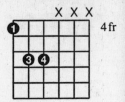

4 fr

AbEbAb

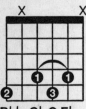

11 fr

AbEbAb

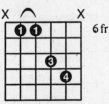

6 fr

EbAbEbAb

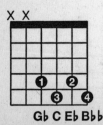

EbAbEbAb

A CHORDS

A MAJOR
[A]

A E A C# E

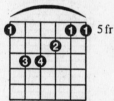

A E A C# E A

X   X
9 fr

C#   C# E A

X X
7 fr

A E A C#

A MINOR
[Am, Ami, A-]

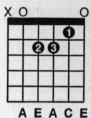

A E A C

5 fr

A E A C E A

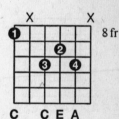

X   X
8 fr

C   C E A

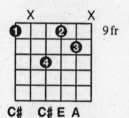

X X
7 fr

A E A C

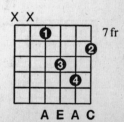

114

A AUGMENTED
[A+, Aaug, A(#5)]

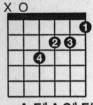

A E# A C# E#

C# E# A C#

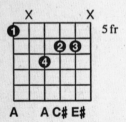
5 fr

A   A C# E#

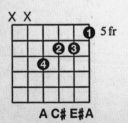
5 fr

A C# E# A

A SUSPENDED FOURTH
[Asus, Asus4]

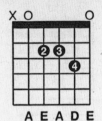

A E A D E

5 fr

A D A D E A

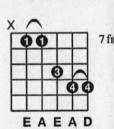
7 fr

E A E A D

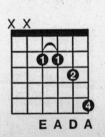

E A D A

A SIXTH
[A6]

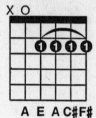

A E A C#F#

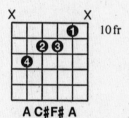

10 fr

A C#F# A

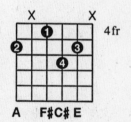

4 fr

A   F#C# E

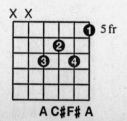

5 fr

A C#F# A

A MINOR SIXTH
[Am6, Ami6, A-6]

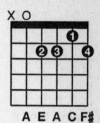

A E A C F#

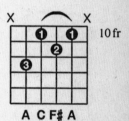

10 fr

A C F# A

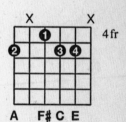

4 fr

A   F#C E

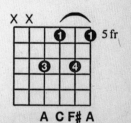

5 fr

A C F# A

A SEVENTH
[A7]

A E G C# E

5 fr

A E G C# E A

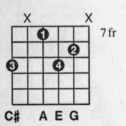

7 fr

C#   A E G

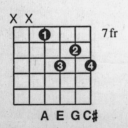

7 fr

A E G C#

A MAJOR SEVENTH
[Amaj7, AMA7, A△7]

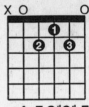

A E G# C# E

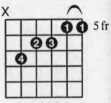

5 fr

E G# C# E A

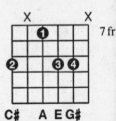

7 fr

C#   A E G#

4 fr

A C# E G#

117

A MINOR SEVENTH
[Am7, AMI7, A-7]

A MINOR MAJOR SEVENTH
[Am(maj7), Am#7]

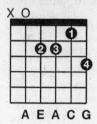

A E A C G

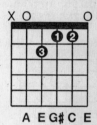

A E G# C E

A E G C E A

A E G# C E A

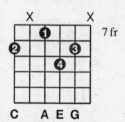

C   A E G

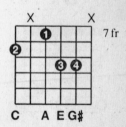

C   A E G#

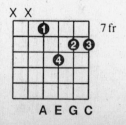

A E G C

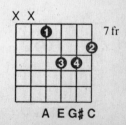

A E G# C

A MINOR SEVENTH FLATTED FIFTH

[Am7♭5, Ami7♭5, A-7♭5, A♯7]

A E♭ G C

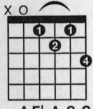

A E♭ A C G

A   G C E♭

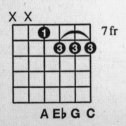

7 fr

A E♭ G C

A DIMINISHED SEVENTH

[Adim7, A°7, Adim]

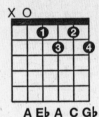

A E♭ A C G♭

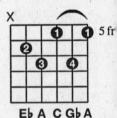

5 fr

E♭ A C G♭ A

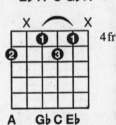

4 fr

A   G♭ C E♭

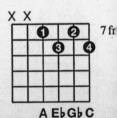

7 fr

A E♭ G♭ C

A SEVENTH SUSPENDED FOURTH

[A7sus, A7sus4]

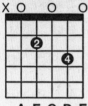

A E G D E

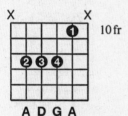

A D G A

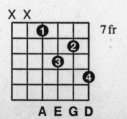

A E G D E A

A E G D

A SEVENTH SHARPED FIFTH

[A7#5, A+7]

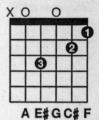

A E# G C# F

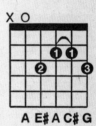

A E# A C# G

A G C# E#

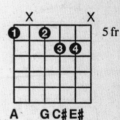

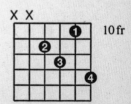

C# G A E#

A NINTH
[A9]

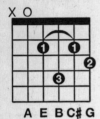

A E B C# G

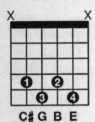

C# G B E

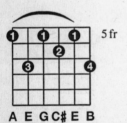

5 fr

A E G C# E B

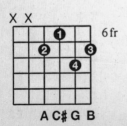

6 fr

A C# G B

A MAJOR NINTH
[Amaj9, AMA9, A△9]

A E B C# G#

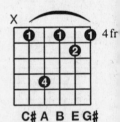

4 fr

C# A B E G#

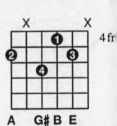

4 fr

A G# B E

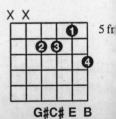

5 fr

G# C# E B

A MINOR NINTH
[Am9, Ami9, A-9]

A ADDED NINTH
[A(add9), A(9), A(add2)]

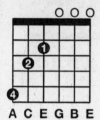

A C E G B E

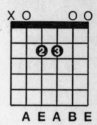

A E A B E

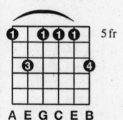

5 fr

A E G C E B

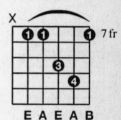

7 fr

E A E A B

C   B E G

C#   B E A

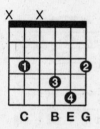

5 fr

G C E B

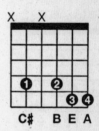

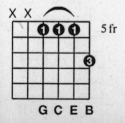

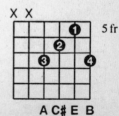

5 fr

A C# E B

122

A SIX NINE

[A6/9, A$_9^6$]

X O

A E B C# F#

X

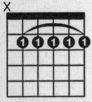

B E A C# F#

X   X

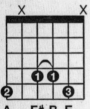

A   F# B E

X X

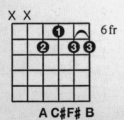
6 fr

A C# F# B

A SEVENTH SHARPED NINTH

[A7#9]

X

B# E A C# G

X   X
11 fr

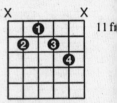

A C# G B#

5 fr

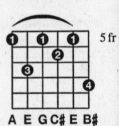

A E G C# E B#

X X
6 fr

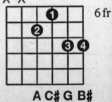

A C# G B#

123

A SEVENTH FLATTED NINTH

[A7♭9]

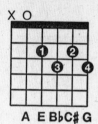

A E B♭C♯ G

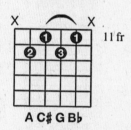

A C♯ G B♭ — 11 fr

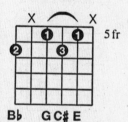

B♭ G C♯ E — 5 fr

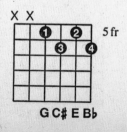

G C♯ E B♭ — 5 fr

A FIFTH

[A5, A(no3)]

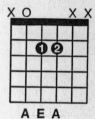

A E A

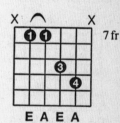

A E A — 5 fr

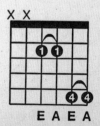

E A E A — 7 fr

E A E A

Bb CHORDS

Bb and A# are enharmonically equivalent. For the sake of convenience, all chords have been notated as Bb chords.

Bb MAJOR
[Bb]

Bb F Bb D

6 fr

Bb F Bb D F Bb

8 fr

D Bb F Bb

8 fr

Bb F Bb D

Bb MINOR
[Bbm, Bbmi, Bb-]

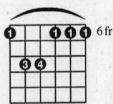

Bb F BbDb F

6 fr

Bb F BbDb F Bb

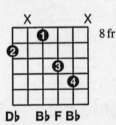

8 fr

Db Bb F Bb

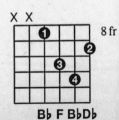

8 fr

Bb F BbDb

Bb AUGMENTED
[Bb+, Bbaug, Bb(#5)]

Bb SUSPENDED FOURTH
[Bbsus, Bbsus4]

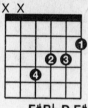

F#Bb D F#

Bb F BbEb

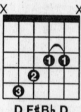

D F#Bb D

BbEbBbEb F Bb

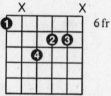

6 fr

Bb   Bb D F#

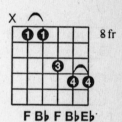

8 fr

F Bb F BbEb

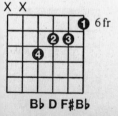

6 fr

Bb D F#Bb

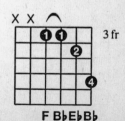

3 fr

F BbEbBb

Bb SIXTH
[Bb6]

Bb MINOR SIXTH
[Bbm6, Bbmi6, Bb-6]

Bb F Bb D G

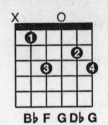

Bb F G Db G

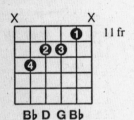

11 fr

Bb D G Bb

6 fr

Bb F Bb Db G Bb

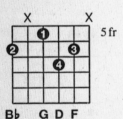

5 fr

Bb G D F

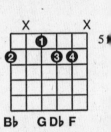

5 fr

Bb G Db F

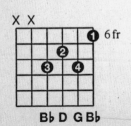

6 fr

Bb D G Bb

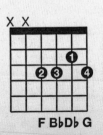

F Bb Db G

Bb SEVENTH
[Bb7]

Bb F Ab D F

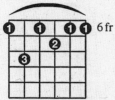

6 fr

Bb F Ab D F Bb

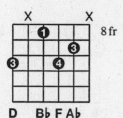

8 fr

D   Bb F Ab

F Bb D Ab

Bb MAJOR SEVENTH
[Bbmaj7, BbMA7, Bb△7]

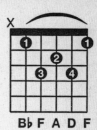

Bb F A D F

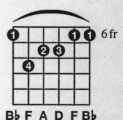

6 fr

Bb F A D F Bb

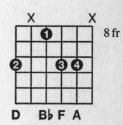

8 fr

D   Bb F A

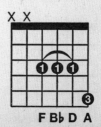

F Bb D A

Bb MINOR SEVENTH
[Bbm7, Bbmi7, Bb-7]

Bb MINOR MAJOR SEVENTH
[Bbm(maj7), Bbm#7]

Bb F Ab Db F

Bb F A Db F

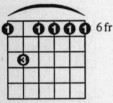

Bb F Ab Db F Bb

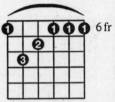

Bb F A Db F Bb

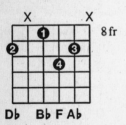

Db Bb F Ab

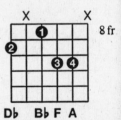

Db Bb F A

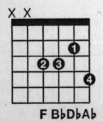

F Bb Db Ab

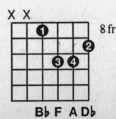

Bb F A Db

Bb MINOR SEVENTH FLATTED FIFTH

[Bbm7b5, Bbmi7b5, Bb-7b5, Bb#7]

Bb DIMINISHED SEVENTH

[Bbdim7, Bb°7, Bbdim]

Bb Fb Ab Db

Bb Fb Abb Db Fb

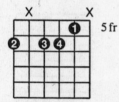

Bb Ab Db Fb

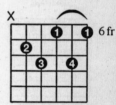

Fb Bb Db Abb Bb

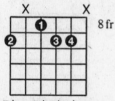

Db Bb Fb Ab

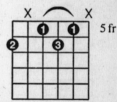

Bb Abb Db Fb

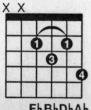

Fb Bb Db Ab

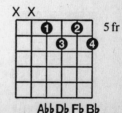

Abb Db Fb Bb

Bb SEVENTH SUSPENDED FOURTH
[Bb7sus, Bb7sus4]

Bb F Ab Eb F

6 fr

Bb F Ab Eb F Bb

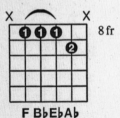

8 fr

F Bb Eb Ab

F Bb Eb Ab

Bb SEVENTH SHARPED FIFTH
[Bb7#5, Bb+7]

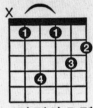

Bb F# Ab D F#

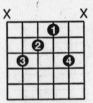

7 fr

F# Bb D Ab

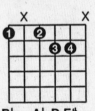

6 fr

Bb Ab D F#

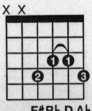

F# Bb D Ab

Bb NINTH
[Bb9]

Bb D Ab C F

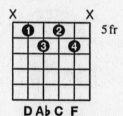

5 fr

D Ab C F

6 fr

Bb F Ab D F C

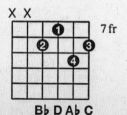

7 fr

Bb D Ab C

Bb MAJOR NINTH
[Bbmaj9, BbMA9, Bb△9]

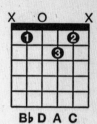

Bb D A C

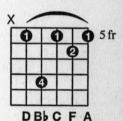

5 fr

D Bb C F A

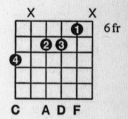

6 fr

C   A D F

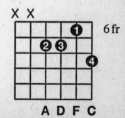

6 fr

A D F C

Bb MINOR NINTH
[Bbm9, Bbmi9, Bb-9]

Bb ADDED NINTH
[Bb(add9), Bb(9), Bb(add2)]

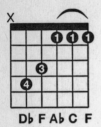

Db F Ab C F

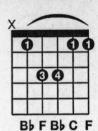

Bb F Bb C F

Bb F AbDb F C

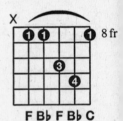

F Bb F Bb C

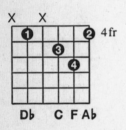

Db C F Ab

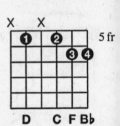

D C F Bb

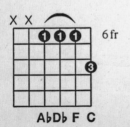

AbDb F C

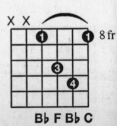

Bb F Bb C

Bb SIX NINE

[Bb6/9, Bb$^6_9$]

Bb SEVENTH SHARPED NINE

[Bb7#9]

Bb D G C F

Bb D Ab C#

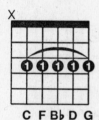

C F Bb D G

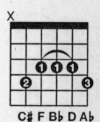

C# F Bb D Ab

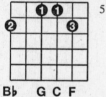

5 fr

Bb   G C F

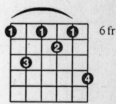

6 fr

Bb F Ab D F C#

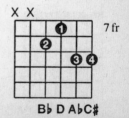

7 fr

Bb D G C

7 fr

Bb D Ab C#

Bb SEVENTH FLATTED NINE

[Bb7b9]

Bb D Ab Cb F

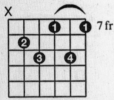
7 fr

F Cb D Ab Cb

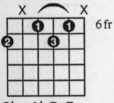
6 fr

Cb Ab D F

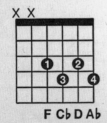

F Cb D Ab

Bb FIFTH

[Bb5, Bb(no3)]

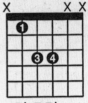

Bb F Bb

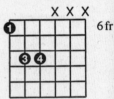
6 fr

Bb F Bb

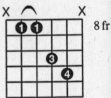
8 fr

F Bb F Bb

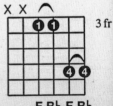
3 fr

F Bb F Bb

B CHORDS

B MAJOR
[B]

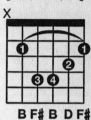

B F# B D#

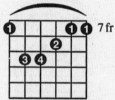

B F# B D#F# B

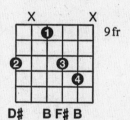

D# B F# B

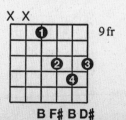

B F# B D#

B MINOR
[Bm, Bmi, B-]

B F# B D F#

B F# B D F# B

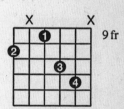

D B F# B

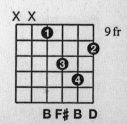

B F# B D

B AUGMENTED
[B+, Baug, B(#5)]

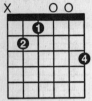

B D# F✕ B F✕

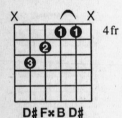

4 fr

D# F✕ B D#

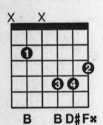

B　　B D# F✕

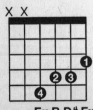

F✕ B D# F✕

B SUSPENDED FOURTH
[Bsus, Bsus4]

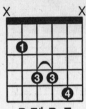

B F# B E

7 fr

B E B E F# B

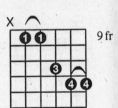

9 fr

F# B F# B E

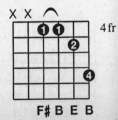

4 fr

F# B E B

B SIXTH
[B6]

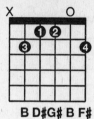

B D#G# B F#

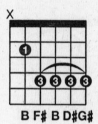

B F# B D#G#

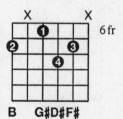

B G#D#F#

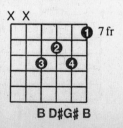

B D#G# B

B MINOR SIXTH
[Bm6, Bmi6, B-6]

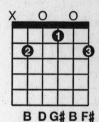

B DG# B F#

B F# B DG# B

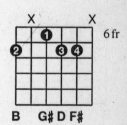

B G# D F#

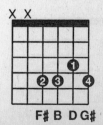

F# B DG#

B SEVENTH
[B7]

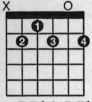

B D# A B F#

B F# A D#F#

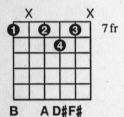

7 fr

B   A D#F#

F# B D# A

B MAJOR SEVENTH
[Bmaj7, BMA7, B△7]

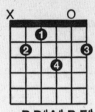

B D#A# B F#

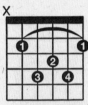

B F#A#D#F#

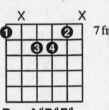

7 fr

B   A#D#F#

4 fr

F# B D#A#

B MINOR SEVENTH
[Bm7, Bmi7, B-7]

B MINOR MAJOR SEVENTH
[Bm(maj7), Bm#7]

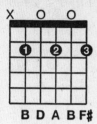

B D A B F#

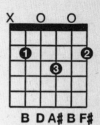

B D A# B F#

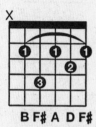

B F# A D F#

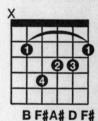

B F# A# D F#

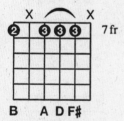

7 fr

B   A D F#

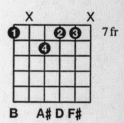

7 fr

B   A# D F#

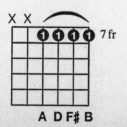

7 fr

A D F# B

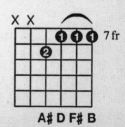

7 fr

A# D F# B

B MINOR SEVENTH FLATTED FIFTH

[Bm7♭5, Bmi7♭5, B-7♭5, B♥7]

B D A B F

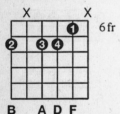

B F A D

6 fr

B A D F

B F A D

9 fr

B DIMINISHED SEVENTH

[Bdim7, B°7, Bdim]

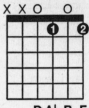

D A♭ B F

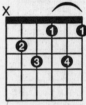

B F A♭ D F

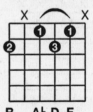

6 fr

B A♭ D F

A♭ D F B

6 fr

B SEVENTH SUSPENDED FOURTH

[B7sus, B7sus4]

B SEVENTH SHARPED FIFTH

[B7#5, B+7]

B E A B E

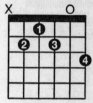

B D# A B F✕

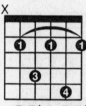

B F# A E F#

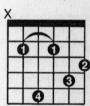

B F✕ A D# F✕

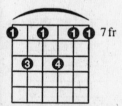

B F# A E F# B — 7 fr

B A D# F✕ — 7 fr

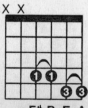

F# B E A

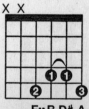

F✕ B D# A

B NINTH
[B9]

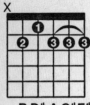

B D# A C#F#

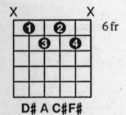

D# A C#F# 6 fr

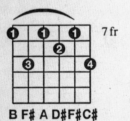

B F# A D#F#C# 7 fr

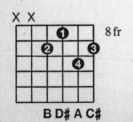

B D# A C# 8 fr

B MAJOR NINTH
[Bmaj9, BMA9, BΔ9]

B D#A#C#

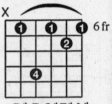

D# B C#F#A# 6 fr

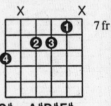

C# A#D#F# 7 fr

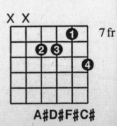

A#D#F#C# 7 fr

B MINOR NINTH
[Bm9, Bmi9, B-9]

B ADDED NINTH
[B(add9), B(9), B(add2)]

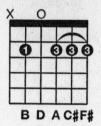

B D A C#F#

B F# B C#F#

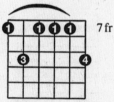

B F# A D F#C#   7 fr

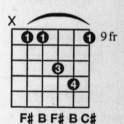

F# B F# B C#   9 fr

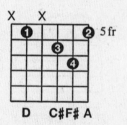

D   C#F# A   5 fr

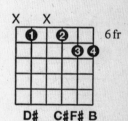

D#   C#F# B   6 fr

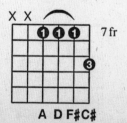

A D F#C#   7 fr

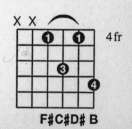

F#C#D# B   4 fr

144

B SIX NINE

[B6/9, B$_9^6$]

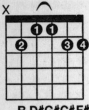

B D#G#C#F#

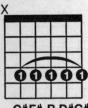

C#F# B D#G#

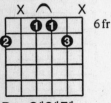

6 fr

B   G#C#F#

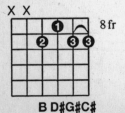

8 fr

B D#G#C#

B SEVENTH SHARPED NINTH

[B7#9]

B D# A C✗

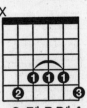

C✗F# B D# A

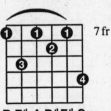

7 fr

B F# A D#F# C✗

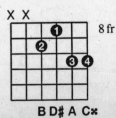

8 fr

B D# A C✗

145

B SEVENTH FLATTED NINTH

[B7♭9]

B D♯ A C

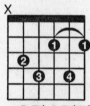

C F♯ A D♯ F♯

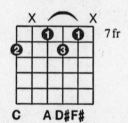

7 fr

C A D♯ F♯

A D♯ F♯ C

7 fr

B FIFTH

[B5, B(no3)]

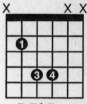

B F♯ B

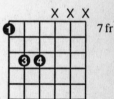

7 fr

B F♯ B

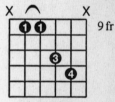

9 fr

F♯ B F♯ B

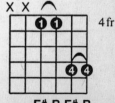

4 fr

F♯ B F♯ B

KEYBOARD CHORDS

The chords in this section of the book can be played on the keyboard using either the right hand or the left hand. Each chord is shown in several different positions, or *inversions*. *Root position* has the root of the chord on the bottom (except in ninth chords, where the third is on the bottom). Each successive inversion takes the bottom note and transposes it up an octave to the top of the chord, leaving the next highest note at the bottom.

C CHORDS

C MAJOR
[C]

C MINOR
[Cm, CMI, C-]

Root Position

Root Position

1st Inversion

1st Inversion

2nd Inversion

2nd Inversion

C AUGMENTED
[C+, Caug, C(#5)]

C SUSPENDED FOURTH
[Csus, Csus4]

Root Position

Root Position

1st Inversion

1st Inversion

2nd Inversion

2nd Inversion

C SIXTH
[C6]

C MINOR SIXTH
[Cm6, CMI6, C-6]

Root Position

Root Position

1st Inversion

1st Inversion

2nd Inversion

2nd Inversion

3rd Inversion

3rd Inversion

C SEVENTH
[C7]

Root Position

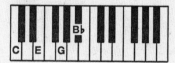

1st Inversion

2nd Inversion

3rd Inversion

C MAJOR SEVENTH
[Cmaj7, CMA7, C△7]

Root Position

1st Inversion

2nd Inversion

3rd Inversion

C MINOR SEVENTH
[Cm7, CMI7, C-7]

C MINOR, MAJOR
SEVENTH
[Cm(maj7), Cm♯7]

Root Position

Root Position

1st Inversion

1st Inversion

2nd Inversion

2nd Inversion

3rd Inversion

3rd Inversion

C SEVENTH, SUSPENDED FOURTH
[C7sus, C7sus4]

C SEVENTH, SHARPED FIFTH
[C7#5, C+7]

Root Position

Root Position

1st Inversion

1st Inversion

2nd Inversion

2nd Inversion

3rd Inversion

3rd Inversion

C DIMINISHED SEVENTH
[Cdim7, C°7, Cdim]

C MINOR SEVENTH, FLATTED FIFTH
[Cm7♭5, CMI7♭5, C-7♭5, C♯7]

Root Position

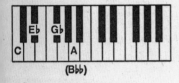

(B♭♭)

Root Position

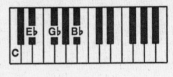

1st Inversion

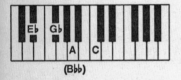

(B♭♭)

1st Inversion

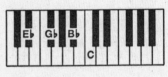

2nd Inversion

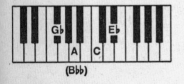

(B♭♭)

2nd Inversion

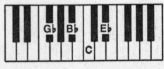

3rd Inversion

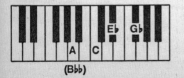

(B♭♭)

3rd Inversion

C NINTH*
[C9]

C MAJOR NINTH*
[Cmaj9, CMA9, C△9]

Root Position

Root Position

1st Inversion

1st Inversion

2nd Inversion

2nd Inversion

3rd Inversion

3rd Inversion

*These ninth chords do not include the root, which is assumed to be played in the bass.

C MINOR NINTH*
[Cm9, CMI9, C-9]

C ADDED NINTH
[C(add9), C(9), C(add2)]

Root Position

Root Position

1st Inversion

1st Inversion

2nd Inversion

2nd Inversion

3rd Inversion

3rd Inversion

*This ninth chord does not include the root, which is assumed to be played in the bass.

D♭/C♯ CHORDS

D♭ and C♯ are enharmonically equivalent. For convenience' sake, all chords have been notated as D♭ chords.

D♭ MAJOR
[D♭]

D♭ MINOR
[D♭m, D♭MI, D♭-]

Root Position

Root Position

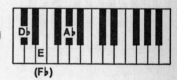

1st Inversion

1st Inversion

2nd Inversion

2nd Inversion

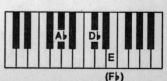

Db AUGMENTED
[Db+, Dbaug, Db(#5)]

Db SUSPENDED FOURTH
[Dbsus, Dbsus4]

Root Position

Root Position

1st Inversion

1st Inversion

2nd Inversion

2nd Inversion

Db SIXTH
[Db6]

Db MINOR SIXTH
[Dbm6, DbMI6, Db-6]

Root Position

Root Position

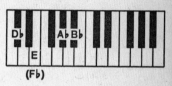

(Fb)

1st Inversion

1st Inversion

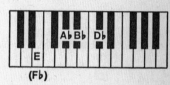

(Fb)

2nd Inversion

2nd Inversion

(Fb)

3rd Inversion

3rd Inversion

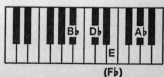

(Fb)

Db SEVENTH
[Db7]

Db MAJOR SEVENTH
[Dbmaj7, DbMA7, Db△7]

Root Position

Root Position

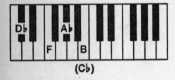

1st Inversion

1st Inversion

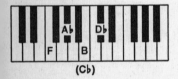

2nd Inversion

2nd Inversion

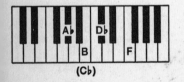

3rd Inversion

3rd Inversion

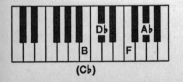

Db MINOR SEVENTH
[Dbm7, DbMI7, Db-7]

Db MINOR, MAJOR
SEVENTH
[Dbm(maj7), Dbm#7]

Root Position

Root Position

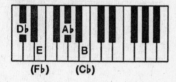

1st Inversion

1st Inversion

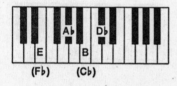

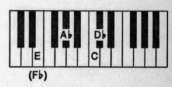

2nd Inversion

2nd Inversion

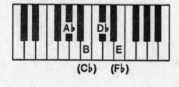

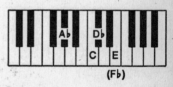

3rd Inversion

3rd Inversion

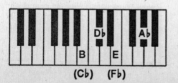

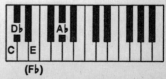

Db SEVENTH, SUSPENDED FOURTH
[Db7sus, Db7sus4]

Root Position

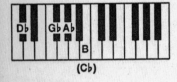

(Cb)

1st Inversion

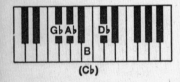

(Cb)

2nd Inversion

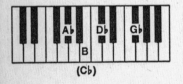

(Cb)

3rd Inversion

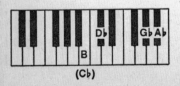

(Cb)

Db SEVENTH, SHARPED FIFTH
[Db7#5, Db+7]

Root Position

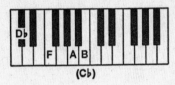

(Cb)

1st Inversion

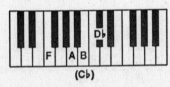

(Cb)

2nd Inversion

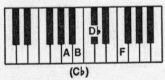

(Cb)

3rd Inversion

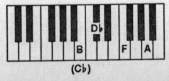

(Cb)

Db DIMINISHED SEVENTH
[Db dim7, Db°7, Db dim]

Db MINOR SEVENTH, FLATTED FIFTH
[Db m7b5, Db MI7b5, Db-7b5, Db∅7]

Root Position

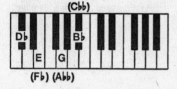

Root Position

1st Inversion

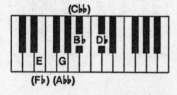

1st Inversion

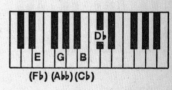

2nd Inversion

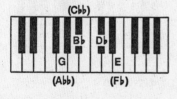

2nd Inversion

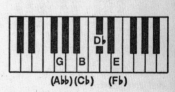

3rd Inversion

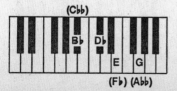

3rd Inversion

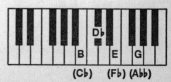

Db NINTH*
[Db9]

Db MAJOR NINTH*
[Dbmaj9, DbMA9, Db△9]

Root Position

Root Position

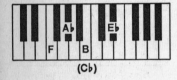

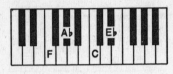

1st Inversion

1st Inversion

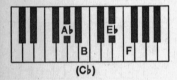

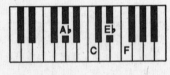

2nd Inversion

2nd Inversion

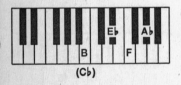

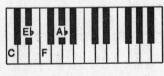

3rd Inversion

3rd Inversion

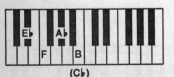

These ninth chords do not include the root, which is assumed to be played in the bass.

Db MINOR NINTH*
[Dbm9, DbMI9, Db-9]

Db ADDED NINTH
[Db(add9), Db(9), Db(add2)]

Root Position

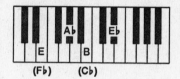

1st Inversion

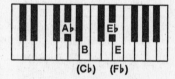

1st Inversion

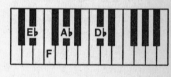

2nd Inversion

2nd Inversion

3rd Inversion

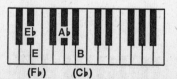

3rd Inversion

*This ninth chord does not include the root, which is assumed to be played in the bass.

D CHORDS

D MAJOR
[D]

D MINOR
[Dm, DMI, D-]

Root Position

Root Position

1st Inversion

1st Inversion

2nd Inversion

2nd Inversion

D AUGMENTED
[D+, Daug, D(#5)]

D SUSPENDED FOURTH
[Dsus, Dsus4]

Root Position

Root Position

1st Inversion

1st Inversion

2nd Inversion

2nd Inversion

D SIXTH
[D6]

D MINOR SIXTH
[Dm6, DMI6, D-6]

Root Position

Root Position

1st Inversion

1st Inversion

2nd Inversion

2nd Inversion

3rd Inversion

3rd Inversion

D SEVENTH
[D7]

D MAJOR SEVENTH
[Dmaj7, DMA7, D△7]

Root Position

Root Position

1st Inversion

1st Inversion

2nd Inversion

2nd Inversion

3rd Inversion

3rd Inversion

D MINOR SEVENTH
[Dm7, DMI7, D-7]

D MINOR, MAJOR
SEVENTH
[Dm(maj7), Dm#7]

Root Position

Root Position

1st Inversion

1st Inversion

2nd Inversion

2nd Inversion

3rd Inversion

3rd Inversion

D SEVENTH, SUSPENDED FOURTH [D7sus, D7sus4]

D SEVENTH, SHARPED FIFTH [D7#5, D+7]

Root Position

Root Position

1st Inversion

1st Inversion

2nd Inversion

2nd Inversion

3rd Inversion

3rd Inversion

D DIMINISHED SEVENTH
[Ddim7, D°7, Ddim]

D MINOR SEVENTH, FLATTED FIFTH
[Dm7♭5, DMI7♭5, D-7♭5, D♯7]

Root Position

Root Position

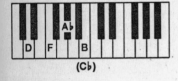
(C♭)

1st Inversion

1st Inversion

(C♭)

2nd Inversion

2nd Inversion

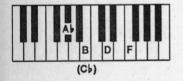
(C♭)

3rd Inversion

3rd Inversion

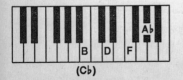
(C♭)

D NINTH*
[D9]

Root Position

1st Inversion

2nd Inversion

3rd Inversion

D MAJOR NINTH*
[Dmaj9, DMA9, D△9]

Root Position

1st Inversion

2nd Inversion

3rd Inversion

These ninth chords do not include the root, which is assumed to be played in the bass.

D MINOR NINTH*
[Dm9, DMI9, D-9]

Root Position

1st Inversion

2nd Inversion

3rd Inversion

D ADDED NINTH
[D(add9), D(9), D(add2)]

Root Position

1st Inversion

2nd Inversion

3rd Inversion

*This ninth chord does not include the root, which is assumed to be played in the bass.

E♭/D♯ CHORDS

E♭ and D♯ are enharmonically equivalent. For convenience' sake, all chords have been notated as E♭ chords.

E♭ MAJOR
[E♭]

E♭ MINOR
[E♭m, E♭MI, E♭-]

Root Position

Root Position

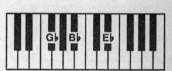

1st Inversion

1st Inversion

2nd Inversion

2nd Inversion

Eb AUGMENTED
[Eb+, Ebaug, Eb(#5)]

Eb SUSPENDED FOURTH
[Ebsus, Ebsus4]

Root Position

Root Position

1st Inversion

1st Inversion

2nd Inversion

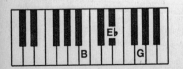

2nd Inversion

Eb SIXTH
[Eb6]

Eb MINOR SIXTH
[Ebm6, EbMI6, Eb-6]

Root Position

Root Position

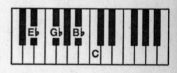

1st Inversion

1st Inversion

2nd Inversion

2nd Inversion

3rd Inversion

3rd Inversion

Eb SEVENTH
[Eb7]

Eb MAJOR SEVENTH
[Ebmaj7, EbMA7, Eb△7]

Root Position

Root Position

1st Inversion

1st Inversion

2nd Inversion

2nd Inversion

3rd Inversion

3rd Inversion

Eb MINOR SEVENTH
[Ebm7, EbMI7, Eb-7]

Eb MINOR, MAJOR
SEVENTH
[Ebm(maj7), Ebm#7]

Root Position

Root Position

1st Inversion

1st Inversion

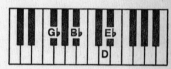

2nd Inversion

2nd Inversion

3rd Inversion

3rd Inversion

Eb SEVENTH, SUSPENDED FOURTH
[Eb7sus, Eb7sus4]

Root Position

1st Inversion

2nd Inversion

3rd Inversion

Eb SEVENTH, SHARPED FIFTH
[Eb7#5, Eb+7]

Root Position

1st Inversion

2nd Inversion

3rd Inversion

Eb DIMINISHED SEVENTH
[Ebdim7, Eb°7, Ebdim]

Eb MINOR SEVENTH, FLATTED FIFTH
[Ebm7b5, EbMI7b5, Eb-7b5, Eb⌀7]

Root Position

(Bbb)(Dbb)

Root Position

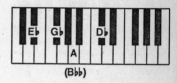

(Bbb)

1st Inversion

(Bbb)(Dbb)

1st Inversion

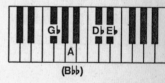

(Bbb)

2nd Inversion

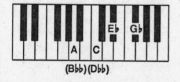

(Bbb)(Dbb)

2nd Inversion

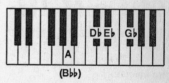

(Bbb)

3rd Inversion

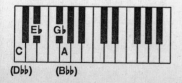

(Dbb)   (Bbb)

3rd Inversion

(Bbb)

E♭ NINTH*
[E♭9]

E♭ MAJOR NINTH*
[E♭maj9, E♭MA9, E♭△9]

Root Position

Root Position

1st Inversion

1st Inversion

2nd Inversion

2nd Inversion

3rd Inversion

3rd Inversion

These ninth chords do not include the root, which is assumed to be played in the bass.

Eb MINOR NINTH*
[Ebm9, EbMI9, Eb-9]

Eb ADDED NINTH
[Eb(add9), Eb(9), Eb(add2)]

Root Position

Root Position

1st Inversion

1st Inversion

2nd Inversion

2nd Inversion

3rd Inversion

3rd Inversion

*This ninth chord does not include the root, which is assumed to be played in the bass.

E CHORDS

E MAJOR
[E]

E MINOR
[Em, EMI, E-]

Root Position

Root Position

1st Inversion

1st Inversion

2nd Inversion

2nd Inversion

E AUGMENTED
[E+, Eaug, E(♯5)]

E SUSPENDED FOURTH
[Esus, Esus4]

Root Position

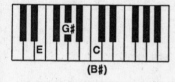

Root Position

1st Inversion

1st Inversion

2nd Inversion

2nd Inversion

E SIXTH
[E6]

E MINOR SIXTH
[Em6, EMI6, E-6]

Root Position

Root Position

1st Inversion

1st Inversion

2nd Inversion

2nd Inversion

3rd Inversion

3rd Inversion

E SEVENTH
[E7]

E MAJOR SEVENTH
[Emaj7, EMA7, E△7]

Root Position

Root Position

1st Inversion

1st Inversion

2nd Inversion

2nd Inversion

3rd Inversion

3rd Inversion

E MINOR SEVENTH
[Em7, EMI7, E-7]

E MINOR, MAJOR
SEVENTH
[Em(maj7), Em#7]

Root Position

Root Position

1st Inversion

1st Inversion

2nd Inversion

2nd Inversion

3rd Inversion

3rd Inversion

E SEVENTH, SUSPENDED FOURTH
[E7sus, E7sus4]

Root Position

1st Inversion

2nd Inversion

3rd Inversion

E SEVENTH, SHARPED FIFTH
[E7#5, E+7]

Root Position

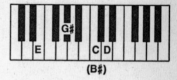

1st Inversion

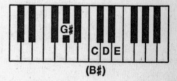

2nd Inversion

3rd Inversion

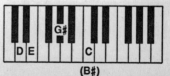

E DIMINISHED SEVENTH
[Edim7, E°7, Edim]

E MINOR SEVENTH,
FLATTED FIFTH
[Em7♭5, EMI7♭5,
E-7♭5, E⌀7]

Root Position

Root Position

1st Inversion

1st Inversion

2nd Inversion

2nd Inversion

3rd Inversion

3rd Inversion

E NINTH*
[E9]

E MAJOR NINTH*
[Emaj9, EMA9, E△9]

Root Position

Root Position

1st Inversion

1st Inversion

2nd Inversion

2nd Inversion

3rd Inversion

3rd Inversion

*These ninth chords do not include the root, which is assumed to be played in the bass.

E MINOR NINTH*
[Em9, EMI9, E-9]

E ADDED NINTH
[E(add9), E(9), E(add2)]

Root Position

Root Position

1st Inversion

1st Inversion

2nd Inversion

2nd Inversion

3rd Inversion

3rd Inversion

*This ninth chord does not include the root, which is assumed to be played in the bass.

F CHORDS

F MAJOR
[F]

F MINOR
[Fm, FMI, F-]

Root Position

Root Position

1st Inversion

1st Inversion

2nd Inversion

2nd Inversion

F AUGMENTED
[F+, Faug, F(#5)]

F SUSPENDED FOURTH
[Fsus, Fsus4]

Root Position

Root Position

1st Inversion

1st Inversion

2nd Inversion

2nd Inversion

F SIXTH
[F6]

F MINOR SIXTH
[Fm6, FMI6, F-6]

Root Position

Root Position

1st Inversion

1st Inversion

2nd Inversion

2nd Inversion

3rd Inversion

3rd Inversion

F SEVENTH
[F7]

F MAJOR SEVENTH
[Fmaj7, FMA7, F△7]

Root Position

Root Position

1st Inversion

1st Inversion

2nd Inversion

2nd Inversion

3rd Inversion

3rd Inversion

F MINOR SEVENTH
[Fm7, FMI7, F-7]

F MINOR, MAJOR SEVENTH
[Fm(maj7), Fm#7]

Root Position

Root Position

1st Inversion

1st Inversion

2nd Inversion

2nd Inversion

3rd Inversion

3rd Inversion

F SEVENTH, SUSPENDED FOURTH
[F7sus, F7sus4]

F SEVENTH, SHARPED FIFTH
[F7♯5, F+7]

Root Position

Root Position

1st Inversion

1st Inversion

2nd Inversion

2nd Inversion

3rd Inversion

3rd Inversion

F DIMINISHED SEVENTH
[Fdim7, F°7, Fdim]

F MINOR SEVENTH,
FLATTED FIFTH
[Fm7♭5, FMI7♭5,
F-7♭5, F⌀7]

Root Position

Root Position

(C♭) (E♭♭)

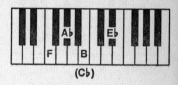

(C♭)

1st Inversion

1st Inversion

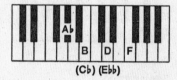

(C♭) (E♭♭)

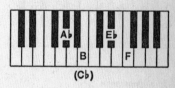

(C♭)

2nd Inversion

2nd Inversion

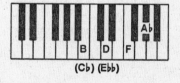

(C♭) (E♭♭)

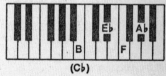

(C♭)

3rd Inversion

3rd Inversion

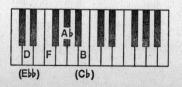

(E♭♭)   (C♭)

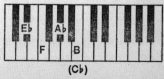

(C♭)

F NINTH*
[F9]

F MAJOR NINTH*
[Fmaj9, FMA9, F△9]

Root Position

Root Position

1st Inversion

1st Inversion

2nd Inversion

2nd Inversion

3rd Inversion

3rd Inversion

These ninth chords do not include the root, which is assumed to be played in the bass.

F MINOR NINTH*
[Fm9, FMI9, F-9]

Root Position

1st Inversion

2nd Inversion

3rd Inversion

F ADDED NINTH
[F(add9), F(9), F(add2)]

Root Position

1st Inversion

2nd Inversion

3rd Inversion

*This ninth chord does not include the root, which is assumed to be played in the bass.

F#/Gb CHORDS

F# and Gb are enharmonically equivalent. For convenience' sake, all chords have been notated as F# chords.

F# MAJOR
[F#]

F# MINOR
[F#m, F#MI, F#-]

Root Position

Root Position

1st Inversion

1st Inversion

2nd Inversion

2nd Inversion

F# AUGMENTED
[F#+, F#aug, F#(#5)]

F# SUSPENDED FOURTH
[F#sus, F#sus4]

Root Position

Root Position

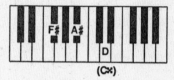

(C×)

1st Inversion

1st Inversion

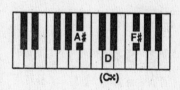

(C×)

2nd Inversion

2nd Inversion

(C×)

F# SIXTH
[F#6]

F# MINOR SIXTH
[F#m6, F#MI6, F#-6]

Root Position

Root Position

1st Inversion

1st Inversion

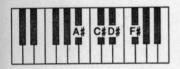

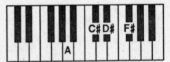

2nd Inversion

2nd Inversion

3rd Inversion

3rd Inversion

F# SEVENTH
[F#7]

F# MAJOR SEVENTH
[F#maj7, F#MA7, F#△7]

Root Position

Root Position

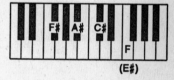

(E#)

1st Inversion

1st Inversion

(E#)

2nd Inversion

2nd Inversion

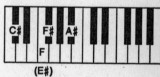

(E#)

3rd Inversion

3rd Inversion

(E#)

F# MINOR SEVENTH
[F#m7, F#MI7, F#-7]

F# MINOR, MAJOR SEVENTH
[F#m(maj7), F#m#7]

Root Position

Root Position

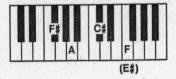

1st Inversion

1st Inversion

2nd Inversion

2nd Inversion

3rd Inversion

3rd Inversion

F# SEVENTH, SUSPENDED FOURTH
[F#7sus, F#7sus4]

Root Position

1st Inversion

2nd Inversion

3rd Inversion

F# SEVENTH, SHARPED FIFTH
[F#7#5, F#+7]

Root Position

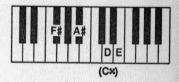

1st Inversion

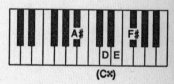

2nd Inversion

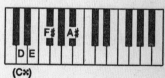

3rd Inversion

F# DIMINISHED SEVENTH
[F#dim7, F#°7, F#dim]

F# MINOR SEVENTH,
FLATTED FIFTH
[F#m7♭5, F#MI7♭5,
F#-7♭5, F#ø7]

Root Position

Root Position

1st Inversion

1st Inversion

2nd Inversion

2nd Inversion

3rd Inversion

3rd Inversion

F# NINTH*
[F#9]

F# MAJOR NINTH*
[F#maj9, F#MA9, F#△9]

Root Position

Root Position

1st Inversion

1st Inversion

2nd Inversion

2nd Inversion

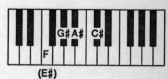

3rd Inversion

3rd Inversion

*These ninth chords do not include the root, which is assumed to be played in the bass.

F# MINOR NINTH*
[F#m9, F#MI9, F#-9]

F# ADDED NINTH
[F#(add9), F#(9), F#(add2)]

Root Position

Root Position

1st Inversion

1st Inversion

2nd Inversion

2nd Inversion

3rd Inversion

3rd Inversion

This ninth chord does not include the root, which is assumed to be played in the bass.

G CHORDS

G MAJOR
[G]

G MINOR
[Gm, GMI, G-]

Root Position

Root Position

1st Inversion

1st Inversion

2nd Inversion

2nd Inversion

G AUGMENTED
[G+, Gaug, G(#5)]

G SUSPENDED FOURTH
[Gsus, Gsus4]

Root Position

Root Position

1st Inversion

1st Inversion

2nd Inversion

2nd Inversion

G SIXTH
[G6]

G MINOR SIXTH
[Gm6, GMI6, G-6]

Root Position

Root Position

1st Inversion

1st Inversion

2nd Inversion

2nd Inversion

3rd Inversion

3rd Inversion

G SEVENTH
[G7]

G MAJOR SEVENTH
[Gmaj7, GMA7, G△7]

Root Position

Root Position

1st Inversion

1st Inversion

2nd Inversion

2nd Inversion

3rd Inversion

3rd Inversion

G MINOR SEVENTH
[Gm7, GMI7, G-7]

G MINOR, MAJOR SEVENTH
[Gm(maj7), Gm#7]

Root Position

Root Position

1st Inversion

1st Inversion

2nd Inversion

2nd Inversion

3rd Inversion

3rd Inversion

G SEVENTH, SUSPENDED FOURTH
[G7sus, G7sus4]

Root Position

1st Inversion

2nd Inversion

3rd Inversion

G SEVENTH, SHARPED FIFTH
[G7♯5, G+7]

Root Position

1st Inversion

2nd Inversion

3rd Inversion

G DIMINISHED SEVENTH
[Gdim7, G°7, Gdim]

G MINOR SEVENTH, FLATTED FIFTH
[Gm7♭5, GMI7♭5, G-7♭5, Gø7]

Root Position

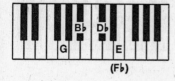

(F♭)

Root Position

1st Inversion

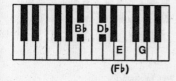

(F♭)

1st Inversion

2nd Inversion

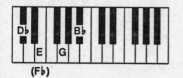

(F♭)

2nd Inversion

3rd Inversion

(F♭)

3rd Inversion

G NINTH*
[G9]

G MAJOR NINTH*
[Gmaj9, GMA9, G△9]

Root Position

Root Position

1st Inversion

1st Inversion

2nd Inversion

2nd Inversion

3rd Inversion

3rd Inversion

These ninth chords do not include the root, which is assumed to be played in the bass.

G MINOR NINTH*
[Gm9, GMI9, G-9]

Root Position

1st Inversion

2nd Inversion

3rd Inversion

G ADDED NINTH
[G(add9), G(9), G(add2)]

Root Position

1st Inversion

2nd Inversion

3rd Inversion

*This ninth chord does not include the root, which is assumed to be played in the bass.

Ab/G# CHORDS

Ab and G# are enharmonically equivalent. For convenience' sake, all chords have been notated as Ab chords.

Ab MAJOR
[Ab]

Ab MINOR
[Abm, AbMI, Ab-]

Root Position

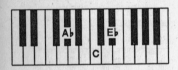

Root Position

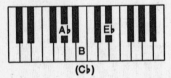

1st Inversion

1st Inversion

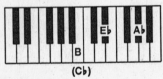

2nd Inversion

2nd Inversion

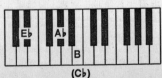

Ab AUGMENTED
[Ab+, Abaug, Ab(#5)]

Ab SUSPENDED FOUR
[Absus, Absus4]

Root Position

Root Position

1st Inversion

1st Inversion

2nd Inversion

2nd Inversion

SIXTH
♭6]

A♭ MINOR SIXTH
[A♭m6, A♭MI6, A♭-6]

Root Position

Root Position

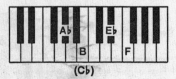
(C♭)

1st Inversion

1st Inversion

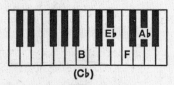
(C♭)

2nd Inversion

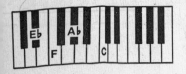

2nd Inversion

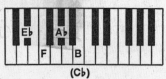
(C♭)

3rd Inversion

3rd Inversion

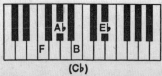
(C♭)

Ab SEVENTH
[Ab7]

Ab MAJOR SEVENTH
[Abmaj7, AbMA7, Ab△7]

Root Position

Root Position

1st Inversion

1st Inversion

2nd Inversion

2nd Inversion

3rd Inversion

3rd Inversion

Ab MINOR SEVENTH
[Abm7, AbMI7, Ab-7]

Ab MINOR, MAJOR
SEVENTH
[Abm(maj7), Abm#7]

Root Position

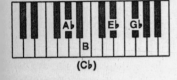

(Cb)

Root Position

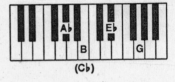

(Cb)

1st Inversion

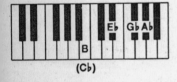

(Cb)

1st Inversion

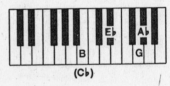

(Cb)

2nd Inversion

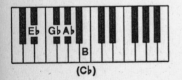

(Cb)

2nd Inversion

(Cb)

3rd Inversion

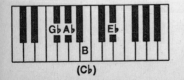

(Cb)

3rd Inversion

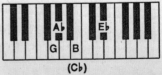

(Cb)

Ab SEVENTH, SUSPENDED FOURTH
[Ab7sus, Ab7sus4]

Root Position

1st Inversion

2nd Inversion

3rd Inversion

Ab SEVENTH, SHARPED FIFTH
[Ab7#5, Ab+7]

Root Position

1st Inversion

2nd Inversion

3rd Inversion

Ab DIMINISHED SEVENTH
[Abdim7, Ab°7, Abdim]

Ab MINOR SEVENTH, FLATTED FIFTH
[Abm7b5, AbMI7b5, Ab-7b5, Abø7]

Root Position

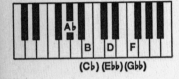

(Cb) (Ebb) (Gbb)

Root Position

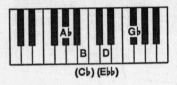

(Cb) (Ebb)

1st Inversion

(Cb) (Ebb) (Gbb)

1st Inversion

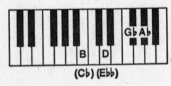

(Cb) (Ebb)

2nd Inversion

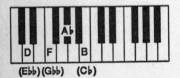

(Ebb) (Gbb)   (Cb)

2nd Inversion

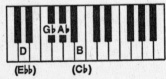

(Ebb)   (Cb)

3rd Inversion

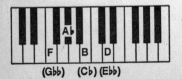

(Gbb)   (Cb) (Ebb)

3rd Inversion

(Cb) (Ebb)

Ab NINTH*
[Ab9]

Root Position

1st Inversion

2nd Inversion

3rd Inversion

Ab MAJOR NINTH*
[Abmaj9, AbMA9, Ab△9]

Root Position

1st Inversion

2nd Inversion

3rd Inversion

These ninth chords do not include the root, which is assumed to be played in the bass.

Ab MINOR NINTH*
[Abm9, AbMI9, Ab-9]

Root Position

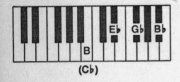

(Cb)

1st Inversion

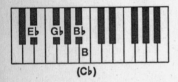

(Cb)

2nd Inversion

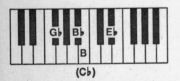

(Cb)

3rd Inversion

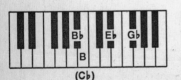

(Cb)

Ab ADDED NINTH
[Ab(add9), Ab(9), Ab(add2)]

Root Position

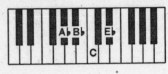

1st Inversion

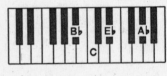

2nd Inversion

3rd Inversion

This ninth chord does not include the root, which is assumed to be played in the bass.

A CHORDS

A MAJOR
[A]

A MINOR
[Am, AMI, A-]

Root Position

Root Position

1st Inversion

1st Inversion

2nd Inversion

2nd Inversion

A AUGMENTED
[A+, Aaug, A(#5)]

A SUSPENDED FOURTH
[Asus, Asus4]

Root Position

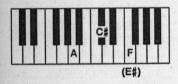

Root Position

1st Inversion

1st Inversion

2nd Inversion

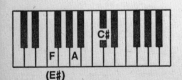

2nd Inversion

A SIXTH
[A6]

A MINOR SIXTH
[Am6, AMI6, A-6]

Root Position

Root Position

1st Inversion

1st Inversion

2nd Inversion

2nd Inversion

3rd Inversion

3rd Inversion

A SEVENTH
[A7]

A MAJOR SEVENTH
[Amaj7, AMA7, A△7]

Root Position

Root Position

1st Inversion

1st Inversion

2nd Inversion

2nd Inversion

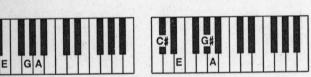

3rd Inversion

3rd Inversion

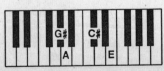

A MINOR SEVENTH
[Am7, AMI7, A-7]

A MINOR, MAJOR
SEVENTH
[Am(maj7), Am#7]

Root Position

Root Position

1st Inversion

1st Inversion

2nd Inversion

2nd Inversion

3rd Inversion

3rd Inversion

A SEVENTH, SUSPENDED FOURTH
[A7sus, A7sus4]

A SEVENTH, SHARPED FIFTH
[A7#5, A+7]

Root Position

Root Position

(E#)

1st Inversion

1st Inversion

(E#)

2nd Inversion

2nd Inversion

(E#)

3rd Inversion

3rd Inversion

(E#)

A DIMINISHED SEVENTH
[Adim7, A°7, Adim]

A MINOR SEVENTH, FLATTED FIFTH
[Am7b5, AMI7b5, A-7b5, Aᵒ7]

Root Position

Root Position

1st Inversion

1st Inversion

2nd Inversion

2nd Inversion

3rd Inversion

3rd Inversion

A NINTH*
[A9]

A MAJOR NINTH*
[Amaj9, AMA9, A△9]

Root Position

Root Position

1st Inversion

1st Inversion

2nd Inversion

2nd Inversion

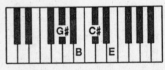

3rd Inversion

3rd Inversion

These ninth chords do not include the root, which is assumed to be played in the bass.

A MINOR NINTH*
[Am9, AMI9, A-9]

A ADDED NINTH
[A(add9), A(9), A(add2)]

Root Position

Root Position

1st Inversion

1st Inversion

2nd Inversion

2nd Inversion

3rd Inversion

3rd Inversion

*This ninth chord does not include the root, which is assumed to be played in the bass.

B♭/A♯ CHORDS

B♭ and A♯ are enharmonically equivalent. For convenience' sake, all chords have been notated as B♭ chords.

B♭ MAJOR
[B♭]

B♭ MINOR
[B♭m, B♭MI, B♭-]

Root Position

Root Position

1st Inversion

1st Inversion

2nd Inversion

2nd Inversion

Bb AUGMENTED
[Bb+, Bbaug, Bb(#5)]

Bb SUSPENDED FOURTH
[Bbsus, Bbsus4]

Root Position

Root Position

1st Inversion

1st Inversion

2nd Inversion

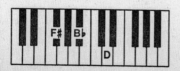

2nd Inversion

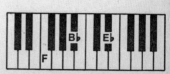

Bb SIXTH
[Bb6]

Bb MINOR SIXTH
[Bbm6, BbMI6, Bb-6]

Root Position

Root Position

1st Inversion

1st Inversion

2nd Inversion

2nd Inversion

3rd Inversion

3rd Inversion

Bb SEVENTH
[Bb7]

Bb MAJOR SEVENTH
[Bbmaj7, BbMA7, Bb△7]

Root Position

Root Position

1st Inversion

1st Inversion

2nd Inversion

2nd Inversion

3rd Inversion

3rd Inversion

Bb MINOR SEVENTH
[Bbm7, BbMI7, Bb-7]

Bb MINOR, MAJOR
SEVENTH
[Bbm(maj7), Bbm#7]

Root Position

Root Position

1st Inversion

1st Inversion

2nd Inversion

2nd Inversion

3rd Inversion

3rd Inversion

Bb SEVENTH, SUSPENDED FOURTH
[Bb7sus, Bb7sus4]

Root Position

1st Inversion

2nd Inversion

3rd Inversion

Bb SEVENTH, SHARPED FIFTH
[Bb7#5, Bb+7]

Root Position

1st Inversion

2nd Inversion

3rd Inversion

Bb DIMINISHED SEVENTH
[Bbdim7, Bb°7, Bbdim]

Bb MINOR SEVENTH, FLATTED FIFTH
[Bbm7b5, BbMI7b5, Bb-7b5, Bbø7]

Root Position

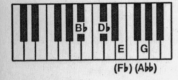

(Fb) (Abb)

Root Position

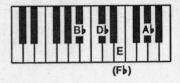

(Fb)

1st Inversion

(Fb) (Abb)

1st Inversion

(Fb)

2nd Inversion

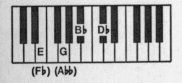

(Fb) (Abb)

2nd Inversion

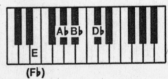

(Fb)

3rd Inversion

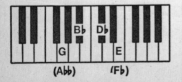

(Abb) (Fb)

3rd Inversion

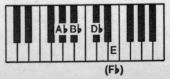

(Fb)

Bb NINTH*
[Bb9]

Root Position

1st Inversion

2nd Inversion

3rd Inversion

Bb MAJOR NINTH*
[Bbmaj9, BbMA9, Bb△9]

Root Position

1st Inversion

2nd Inversion

3rd Inversion

*These ninth chords do not include the root, which is assumed to be played in the bass.

246

Bb MINOR NINTH*
[Bbm9, BbMI9, Bb-9]

Bb ADDED NINTH
[Bb(add9), Bb(9), Bb(add2)]

Root Position

Root Position

1st Inversion

1st Inversion

2nd Inversion

2nd Inversion

3rd Inversion

3rd Inversion

This ninth chord does not include the root, which is assumed to be played in the bass.

B CHORDS

B MAJOR
[B]

B MINOR
[Bm, BMI, B-]

Root Position

Root Position

1st Inversion

1st Inversion

2nd Inversion

2nd Inversion

248

B AUGMENTED
[B+, Baug, B(#5)]

B SUSPENDED FOURTH
[Bsus, Bsus4]

Root Position

Root Position

1st Inversion

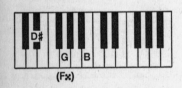

1st Inversion

2nd Inversion

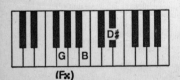

2nd Inversion

B SIXTH
[B6]

B MINOR SIXTH
[Bm6, BMI6, B-6]

Root Position

Root Position

1st Inversion

1st Inversion

2nd Inversion

2nd Inversion

3rd Inversion

3rd Inversion

B SEVENTH
[B7]

B MAJOR SEVENTH
[Bmaj7, BMA7, B△7]

Root Position

Root Position

1st Inversion

1st Inversion

2nd Inversion

2nd Inversion

3rd Inversion

3rd Inversion

B MINOR SEVENTH
[Bm7, BMI7, B-7]

B MINOR, MAJOR
SEVENTH
[Bm(maj7), Bm♯7]

Root Position

Root Position

1st Inversion

1st Inversion

2nd Inversion

2nd Inversion

3rd Inversion

3rd Inversion

B SEVENTH, SUSPENDED FOURTH
[B7sus, B7sus4]

Root Position

1st Inversion

2nd Inversion

3rd Inversion

B SEVENTH, SHARPED FIFTH
[B7#5, B+7]

Root Position

1st Inversion

2nd Inversion

3rd Inversion

B DIMINISHED SEVENTH
[Bdim7, B°7, Bdim]

B MINOR SEVENTH, FLATTED FIFTH
[Bm7♭5, BMI7♭5, B-7♭5, B°7]

Root Position

Root Position

1st Inversion

1st Inversion

2nd Inversion

2nd Inversion

3rd Inversion

3rd Inversion

B NINTH*
[B9]

B MAJOR NINTH*
[Bmaj9, BMA9, B△9]

Root Position

Root Position

1st Inversion

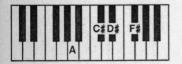

1st Inversion

2nd Inversion

2nd Inversion

3rd Inversion

3rd Inversion

These ninth chords do not include the root, which is assumed to be played in the bass.

B MINOR NINTH*
[Bm9, BMI9, B-9]

B ADDED NINTH
[B(add9), B(9), B(add2)]

Root Position

Root Position

1st Inversion

1st Inversion

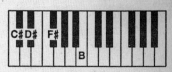

2nd Inversion

2nd Inversion

3rd Inversion

3rd Inversion

This ninth chord does not include the root, which is assumed to be played in the bass.